CW00704175

GEOFF THOMPSON

Everything that Happens to Me is Great

EVERYTHING THAT HAPPENS TO ME IS GREAT

Summersdale Publishers Ltd
46 West Street
Chichester
West Sussex
PO19 1RP
UK

www.summersdale.com

Printed and bound in Great Britain

ISBN: 978-1-84024-684-1

To God, for allowing me to be a conduit for His works, and also for allowing me to experience (every day) the Idyll.

To my beautiful wife Sharon, because she is my works, she is my Idyll.

Also by Geoff Thompson

Red Mist
Watch My Back: The Geoff Thompson Autobiography
The Elephant and the Twig: The Art of Positive Thinking
The Great Escape: The 10 Secrets to Loving Your Life and Living Your Dreams
Fear – The Friend of Exceptional People: Techniques in Controlling Fear
Shape Shifter: Transform Your Life in 1 Day
The Formula: The Secret to a Better Life
Stress Buster: How to Stop Stress from Killing You
Dead or Alive: The Choice is Yours
Everything That Happens to Me is Good
The Beginner's Guide to Darkness

Therefore get up: control your breathlessness
By force of mind, which wins in every battle,
If with its heavy body it does not sink.

You have much longer stairs to climb than these;
It is not enough to leave this lot behind:
If you have understood me, act accordingly.

Dante *The Divine Comedy*

Contents

Preface

Is there anything more exciting than sneaking off to a remote corner of your mind, or of your life (or in my case, a remote corner of a cafe in the Coventry Ikea), with a good book? I have to tell you that for me it is glorious – especially if the book is compact and broken down into bite-sized pieces; easy on the eye, gentle on the digestion. I love a tome as much as the next man. It is very challenging and equally satisfying to ascend a literary Everest once in a while, and I make it my job to do so. It stretches my mind and opens my belief system to all sorts of new and exciting possibilities.

But tomes have a time and a place – normally by my bedside cabinet or next to the deckchair on my perennial cruise around places exotic. The weighty volume is not best suited to an hour's commute from somewhere to somewhere else, or from somewhere else back home again. Neither does it bode well in cafes and canteens, on loo breaks or, for that matter, during stolen moments that afford time for an inspirational snack, but not for a committed and lengthy study.

I have written this book for just such moments. Mostly because it is the kind of book I absolutely love to read when my life offers an hour, but not two, and my soul is looking for honest and immediate direction without exposure to filler or folly (or far too many pages).

This is my second book of articles and I have loved writing (or should I say 'being a conduit for') them both. I love words, and these are some of my favourites. I hope they have fallen into an order that you enjoy in the reading as much as I did in the writing.

Be well.

Geoff Thompson.

Introduction

As you may (or may not) know I love to write, and I love to write prolifically. It is an urgency I feel in my very bones, every day of my life, and if I ever go a day without penning something (anything), I feel somehow incomplete, like a tree that has reaped in from the earth and forgotten to give out through the leaves.

But my need has always puzzled me; why do I write, and why do I write about the things I write about? What is the purpose, other than this innate compulsion?

The questions can be perplexing.

When confusion abounds I always do the same thing: I quiet myself, go inwards and ask the question (why?).

And the question that is sincerely asked will always be answered.

A day or so later I got my reply (a message from God). It came to me via an intuition, much like all the great works that come through me. It suggested that I pick up a copy of the Christian Bible and check out a certain section of Revelations, which I duly did. And this is what it said; 'write what you see here'. The words were simple and direct, and they told me exactly what I needed to hear. They were written in a way which suggested that this life we lead is more of a sojourn, a short trip to some foreign shore, than it is a permanent abode. And that whilst on this fleeting visit it is important that we send letters home, telling of the things we have experienced on our journey, and the things that we have learned from those experiences. This made perfect sense to me. But then that usual, conniving little voice popped up (as it is apt to do) and said, 'Who is going to be interested in anything that you have got to say?'

But the voice is old hat; I have heard it a million times and have long since stopped listening to its negativity. And anyway, the verse had made a strong impression in my mind. It was very convincing, and it would not go away. It got me thinking that perhaps my traveller's notes were important and that I should ignore my nay-saying, egotistical sub-vocalisation and write them anyway. Because people (myself especially) need guidance, and honest notes from an ardent traveller are rare. I should know; I am always looking for direction, continually on the hunt for a word or a phrase that might act as grist or catalyst for my own journey – and I rarely find it.

So here are my notes. They are honest and I hope they help (or at least entertain).

Chapter 1

Are You Where You Want To Be?

It was Christmas. I was sitting with Sharon having a cup of tea and we were preparing to go out for a well-earned (posh) meal. I'd just, one hour since, finished teaching a successful course and I was contemplating what a great day it had been. We'd had two hundred amazing people attend from all over Europe and the atmosphere had been euphoric.

Then the phone rang. It was a friend who ended my reverie with a swift statement.

'Geoff. I'm really sorry to disturb you but... one of the students who was on the course today has died on his way home.'

I can't lie. I was shocked and upset. The news had caught me off guard and I felt it in my very bones.

It turned out that the man in question was driving home and, mid traffic, had experienced a massive heart attack that had killed him instantly. It was a huge shock to his friends and family because he was a fit man with no obvious ailments.

He was a man who loved his motors, and had earned enough in his middle age to treat himself to a particularly nice sports car, the one he had always dreamt of owning. It was in this splendid vehicle that he drove down to the course and, post training, the one in which he tragically spent his dying seconds.

There was little we could do, the ambulance had already collected his body and his wife had been informed. I asked my friend to keep in touch and to let me know if there was anything I could do.

The incident had a profound effect on me. I had experienced death before, of course (four of my friends were murdered during my time as a doorman and I'd also lost my brother tragically), but something about this passing – even though I did not know this lovely man personally – really moved me. It was not so much the death itself, which was sad enough, rather it was the depth of understanding and insight that his wonderful wife had demonstrated on hearing the bad news. What she said changed the way I looked at my life. Despite the grief that her husband's unexpected death had brought her, she said she was strangely happy, because he was in the car he had always wanted to drive, travelling back from a course he had always wanted to attend. She was grateful, she said, because her husband was where he wanted to be when he died.

He was where he wanted to be.

How many people can say that?

How many people can say that their mum, dad, brother, or sister was where they wanted to be when they died?

I had to really think about this, very deeply. Because, if I am honest, I don't know very many people who are where they want to be whilst they are alive, let alone when they die. It really made me think about my own life; was I where I wanted to be? Was I living to my best potential, or was I taking second best and waiting for the right time to change, a time that never seemed to materialise? And was I enjoying the bounty that life had on offer, or was I waiting for some illusive rainy day to enjoy the fruits of my labour?

It forced me to take an inventory of my life. I cleared out all the things that were redundant, and stopped doing all the things that did not make my heart sing.

It was a revealing time.

I could see from my clear out that probably fifty per cent of my life was either redundant baggage or residue (including some of the people). These liabilities took more from me than they returned. They were habits and beliefs past their sell-by date. So I stripped things back to the metal, made myself light and made a point of only engaging in the things that delighted me. It didn't happen overnight. But I got started and I made the changes. I wanted to be in a position in my life so that if tragedy struck unexpectedly (as it is apt to do) and the reaper reaped before my ten-score years or more, those I left behind could be happy in my passing and could say, 'Yea, my dad/ my brother/ my husband/ my son was where he wanted to be.'

Are *you* where you want to be?

Chapter 2

100 Realities (inspired by *The Tibetan Book of the Dead*)

Know this: a small world – one that offers limitation as a staple, one that is surrounded by fear, one that has guards of curtail at every exit – is not reality. Or should I say it *is* reality, but just one of a hundred possible realities.

A small reality is the product of a small, underdeveloped mind.

And also know this: all monsters and madmen and demons and demigods and every demiurge – they come from the mind.

The weak body, the shit job, the poor wage and the putrid future; they come from the mind, too.

Bullies, bad men and ugly folk; trace them back to their source and you will find that they all stem from the mind.

The villain, the vicious, the vapid and the vain-glorious are rotten apples that have fallen from the mind tree.

Depression comes from the mind.

So does the vanquished, and the hemmed-in and the haggard.

The mind is responsible for all.

Don Juan Matus said that our reality is but a single room in a house of a hundred rooms and with training we could learn to access the other ninety-nine. In fact, with training we could actually get out of the house.

The 100 realities come from the mind.

The house comes from the mind.

The realities outside the house all come from the mind.

But the mind is controlled by a gargoyle. The gargoyle is called ego, and ego likes to feast on sense-gluttony. It spoils on food, drink, drugs, pornography, alcohol and noise! And it thrives on limiting beliefs, and doubt and blame.

And small realities.

It likes small, safe realities.

The ego comes from the mind.

So train the mind in the art of austerity and asceticism. These are the anathema of ego – its harbinger of doom.

Foster perfect moderation, adopt self-control and give birth to integrity.

Build your foundation on famished ego, and construct large, expansive, palatial realities.

Once you control the mind you become the architect of all that comes from the mind.

Because… everything comes from the mind.

Chapter 3

The Universe Whispers

I have been a man of inquiry all my life. Ever since I was a child in the school playground I have always believed in the possibility of the impossible. I have always been excited by life's great potential (whilst at the same time being extremely frightened of life's great potential). I was the kid who wanted to climb the highest trees, venture to the farthest points and scrimmage with the biggest risks. Whilst other boys were happy to kick a football around the school playing field, I wanted to score the winning goal for Manchester United in the FA cup. Even if I was unable to do so immediately, I never lost sight of the possibility of greatness. I was exhilarated by life. By its mystery. By its potential. I knew that there was an energy out there (some called this energy God) that wanted to help me, that wanted me to grow, to explore and to excite (myself and others). I felt as though the universe was a benevolent and palpable force that loved me like a parent and wanted to offer me all it had. I felt the universe talking to me, guiding me, encouraging me to be outstanding.

Somewhere between childhood and adolescence I sort of lost contact, and what had once seemed an infinite force suddenly, in adulthood, became a finite world of labour, limitation and depression. I am not sure why or how this happened, though I am pretty sure that it was not conspiratorial. I don't believe that there were people sitting in a room somewhere trying to make life difficult for Geoff Thompson. Rather the opposite in fact. The potential never went away, just my connection with the potential. Infinity never shrank, it was just my perception of things that got smaller as I got older.

All I do know is this: whilst I made my way through a plethora of menial jobs, a young marriage and more depressions than you can shake a stick at, somewhere in the back of my mind was this notion that one day I would reconnect with my Power. I would make my life a work of art and I would do my very best to help others to help themselves to shape their lives into a sculpture worthy of the Tate.

This endeavour is not completely altruistic. I am not trying to be some 'smashing' self-sacrificing bloke who puts himself out just to help others. All of my motives are selfish (or as Charles Handy said, 'proper selfish'), in that before you can help others you first have to help yourself. All service ultimately is self-service because ours is a reciprocal experience: what we give out to others is continually coming back to us. As it says in the Bagahavad Gita, when you water the roots of a tree, you automatically feed all the branches and all the leaves. But you cannot give what you do not have, so having is the first stage of giving. And to give prolifically, one has to take prolifically. You have to be a powerful conduit that can receive God in all His forms, and give God to others in whatever form they find amenable.

This is not religion. My God is not full of wrath. He is not a man in the sky with kind eyes and a beard, neither does he strike a vengeance-stick at the wicked and the wrong. Like the sun, He shines on all.

It is ourselves that we need to defend against. We are our only friend, and we are our only enemy. The blame and the praise all lies with us. God is the abundant material that we have the privilege to work with.

Once you are balanced, you can help others get balanced. Once you are fed, you have the strength to feed others. If you are going to inspire others to go through the narrow gate (many are called, few take the challenge), you'd better make mighty sure, first and foremost, that you have taken the narrow gate yourself.

No one (after all) is going to take advice on diamonds from a brick builder.

To feed ourselves, to take proper advantage of the abundance that is ours, we need to recognise that we can get no help from outside ourselves. All our help must come from within. And if we are to help ourselves we first need to understand ourselves, control and ultimately develop sovereignty over ourselves.

We need to be free. And freedom is not found in a book or a poem or a weekend course with a guru.

Freedom is found when we listen to the whisper of the universe. And when it offers us talents we must (and this is very important) get out there and invest those talents, make them work for us and produce a profit. And in producing that profit we automatically become the embodiment of our message. Saint Francis of Assisi said that we should all preach the Gospel, and if we really need to, use words.

Our success is who we are, not what we say. Our fruits preach the 'word' without a single word ever being spoken.

Chapter 4

Alan Titchmarsh

I always talk about the fact that the universe is a benevolent force that is willing us to reap the abundance that is on offer. And I am always harping on about how nature demonstrates this in technicolour, with every land-crawling and sky-flying creature and with every plant and tree. Examples of abundance are all around us if only we will look.

I am also aware that I might come across at times as a little evangelical in my telling. You will have to forgive this. It is simply because I am so excited about the potential we have as a species to go out there and live the life we want to live, knowing that if we would only turn towards our potential, our potential would run towards us. So in this piece I would like to call in a little help. If you won't listen to me (about nature, about abundance) then I know a man you *will* listen to.

Alan Titchmarsh!

(Who?)

Alan Titchmarsh!

Alan Titchmarsh? Does the garden programme! Has a day-time talk show? Writes books, presents radio and... come on! Everyone knows Alan Titchmarsh.

All right, not everyone knows him. For those who are unfamiliar he is best recognised for his plants and seeds and romantic novels. If you are not immediately inspired to greatness by this example, you will be inspired to greatness by what he had to say on one of his gardening programmes recently (I just happened to stumble upon it whilst channel-hopping one bored afternoon – honestly).

I believe you will be inspired because I was inspired, and greatly so.

Actually, now that I am writing this piece I realise that there is a lot about Alan that is inspiring, not least the fact that he is a massively successful television personality, best-selling novelist and a lovely man by all accounts. You do get the feeling with him that whatever he turns his hand to he will make a success of. And you also get the feeling that he knows something that the rest of us have not yet cottoned onto, and that perhaps that 'something' has been picked up from spending his life working in, with and around nature.

He knows about 'stuff' does Alan Titchmarsh. He knows about stuff that grows. And when people know about stuff that grows… we should listen to them. We should observe and we should learn from them. And that is why I always love the gardening programmes. They tell you a lot more about success than a glut of programmes about budding entrepreneurs and business gurus who spend more time pouting to camera than demonstrating trade acumen. The problem with the latter is that 1) they always have great difficulty articulating their success (as though perhaps they are not quite sure how they made it), and 2) they seem to make more mistakes in business and in life than not.

Nature on the other hand has a one hundred per cent success record. It only ever gets it right.

How good is that?

Who would you rather learn from – a man with an ego the size of a small American state or a plant that simply succeeds, every time, and without all the bells and whistles?

Anyway, I digress. I was talking about Alan Titchmarsh and the time I watched him on a TV gardening programme when he blew my mind with a simple (and yet movingly profound) statement.

Oh, one more thing before I get to that all-important statement. There is another thing that I love about the gardening guru that is Alan T: his passion. He is so passionate about plants that it is positively infectious. If you ever do a dissertation on success principles I can guarantee that in your conclusion you will strongly note that all extremely successful people have an absolute passion for their work. They give you the feeling that they would do it for nothing, they love it so much. If you are massively passionate about your work, success will come, because you will find yourself investing nearly all your time in it.

Back to the programme. Alan was placing a new plant into the ground. He was talking about the importance of the soil and the water and the light and... suddenly he looked at the camera, eyes filled with passion, and he said (something like), 'You know what? This plant wants to grow. It really does want to grow. It will do everything it can to grow. All you have to do is help it along a little.'

And that was it. That is what he said and I loved it because I immediately drew parallels in my own life. I could see that everything, absolutely everything, from a germ to a business venture, wants to grow. It wants to grow. All you have to do is give it a little help (well, perhaps not the germ). Everything on this earth (including us) is a product of this earth, and so everything desperately wants life. It needs water and soil and light (or the equivalents), and it will do most of the growing by itself, but it just needs a bit of a hand.

Your body wants to grow.

Your intellect wants to grow.

Your business wants to grow.

Your marriage wants to grow.

Your spirituality desperately wants to grow.

Everything wants to grow. All you need to do is help it to help itself.

Ignore your body and it will become ill (it may even die). Neglect your business and it will falter quickly, maybe fail. Deny your intellect and watch how quickly the brain atrophies. And your marriage will end with a decree nisi if you do not nurture the love and tend to the lover.

After watching that programme with Alan Titchmarsh my life really transformed, because I started to see everything in the same simple terms; it all wants to grow. So help it, and if you help it, it will grow and grow and... Oh, and of course I forgot the most important factor, one that is often missed when people look at and follow simple soil/ water/ light formulas.

The passion!

Alan didn't say it in so many words but it was 'spoken' with every touch, every gesture and every tender smile: we need to put passion into the mix. Passion in business, in marriage, in art and in life is the light that will take an acorn into an oak, a business into a boom and a small mind into a labyrinthine library.

Chapter 5
Full Stop

The Milky Way is a full stop. It's true. The Milky Way, our galaxy, the place that our planet Earth calls home, is but the size of a full stop (in comparison to the known universe) in a book, at a library with shelves as high as five ceilings and as long as the eye can see.

Now that excites me. It really excites me.

You know why? Because it brings perspective to a world that has gotten way – and I say *way* – out of focus.

We sweat the small stuff. We allow it to become our world, our universe and our galaxy, when really, it is just small stuff. But we allow it to become so big that it clouds the very air we breathe, it smothers our vision and – worst of all – it ruins our bodies and stops us from enjoying the world in which we reside for such a short time.

If (comparatively) the Milky Way is the size of a full stop in a five-hundred-page book in a gargantuan library, how small is the Earth? How small is our continent? How tiny is our country, city, town and street? And how small is the problem that you are currently facing, the one that has set up camp in your mind, the one that is threatening to 'do you in'?

How small is it in comparison to what is really out there?

And your business. You want to grow your business to a £100k turnover, or £500k, or a mill, or a billion, or maybe you'd love to expand overseas, or perhaps you want to float it. But the next step seems too big, insurmountable even. But how big is it really when compared to the size of the universe. Even a £1 billion turnover (in perspective) would disappear inside a grain of sand on Blackpool beach. What seems hopelessly large and impossibly difficult, is often tiny. It is just that we allow it to become (in our mind's eye) much bigger than it actually is. (It is very hard, after all, for the eyes to see clearly what the mind has gotten so out of focus.) If we think it is bigger than it actually is, then it *is* bigger than it actually is. Real or not, we have made it real with our minds. So a good way to break this cycle is to look at the problem that you are now facing (health, relationship, business) and place it into correct perspective within the bigger picture. If it is your health that is the issue, and you think your problems insurmountable, and healing seems a possibility too large to grasp, find an example that is far bigger than yours (universes bigger), one that has already been solved, and use it to spur you on. Be inspired by the likes of Stephen Hawking, who was given, over four decades ago, two years to live by some of the best doctors in the world. Not only did he prove them wrong and survive, but he also went on to shake the very foundations of science with his brilliant insights and discoveries. Read about folk who thought bigger than their depression, their illness and their disability and went on to complete the most amazing feats of endurance and strength.

If you think that turning over half a mill in your business is too big to contemplate, then read about, talk to and visit businesses that are turning over ten million. And if you are already at ten mill and want to expand more, then be inspired by a billion. Be inspired by people who grew their conglomerates from a tiny nurtured seed. Be inspired by people like Richard Branson who started his £1 billion empire with no capital and a phone box for an office. Or John Frieda who revolutionised the hairdressing industry from a standing start, by inventing cutting-edge products. After reading Ayn Rand's amazing book,

The Fountainhead and getting acquainted with the lead character, Roark (whose integrity was faultless), Frieda was inspired to create one of the biggest hairdressing businesses in the world today.

It works on a global level or on a local level. I used to write an article a month for my newsletter. I secretly wanted to write one a week but I always felt that writing one really good article a week was a bit too much of a challenge (what with all the other plates I was spinning), until my friend John Harrison told me that he intended to write one article a day for his blog. One a day! Suddenly, one a month seemed lazy and one a week seemed positively achievable. So now I write one a week, and maybe later I will go for one a day (so watch your back young John Harrison, I am coming for your title).

There are examples out there ready for you to find that will put your problems (or what the Chinese would call 'opportunities') into perspective. And when the perspective changes, the world will change with it. What seems massive today will be very manageable tomorrow, and tomorrow's goals will seem positively minute – perhaps the size of a full stop in a book of five-hundred pages – compared to what you will be achieving in a year's time.

Chapter 6

The Stairway of Saturn

I read a great article the other day and I thought I might share the essence of it with you. It was talking about success, the nature of success and what success actually is (because it appears to be different things to different people). What became evident after reading several paragraphs, which had been written by a handful of successful (but very different) folk from completely disparate backgrounds, was that whilst each had their own unique theories on how to become successful, none – not a one – could pinpoint what it actually was that took them from near obscurity to massive success. One man talked about the need for a strong intention, another mentioned integrity, someone else suggested that passion was the vital ingredient, another felt that he tithed his way to success and many more believed that it was all down to good old-fashioned luck; they just happened to be in the right place at the right time.

For every strong theory on success there was an equally attractive and convincing anti-theory that blew the former out of the water.

The reason I think it is hard to write a convincing theory on success is because success usually happens to people when they least expect it, often after arduous years of dedicated and relentless work with no result, and sometimes without any obvious investment. The architect Richard Rogers, for instance, had a desperate period of three years without any work at all. Things had become so difficult that he decided he was probably going to be a failure as an architect so he started teaching at UCLA instead. His project architect at the time, a man called John Tang, was equally desperate, so much so that he was planning to do the Knowledge training and become a London cabby, just to put bread on the table. Then, when all seemed lost, they won a competition to build the Lloyd's building, recognised now as one of the most important pieces of contemporary architecture in the world. One minute these amazing architects could not find enough work to eat, the next they found themselves on the world stage with more work than either of them could cope with.

Personally, my journey has shown me (and I have always believed) that success is a matter of very strong intent coupled with massive tenacity. Staying power is all important. If you are prepared to never ever give in, it will happen. What I can't tell you, what no one can tell you, is when it will happen. Having myself written many books filled with tips, ideas and hard-won beliefs on how to be successful, and having read hundreds of other books by some of the most impressive men and women of our species, I have discovered that no one seems able to articulate what it is that creates the tipping point we all need to take us from aspirants of success to embodiments of success. Then I read an interesting article about the beautiful actress, Joanna Lumley and it really helped to shed light on the issue. I think it offers hope to all the people out there who might be struggling to make their mark, thinking that the door to success will never open for them. The interviewer was asking the standard question, 'How did you succeed?' and probably expected an answer along the lines of, 'The key is this, that or the other.' What she got instead was refreshing, inspiring and very revealing. Joanna explained that she had been working as a model, and then as an actress for quite some years, trying to make a break in to what can be a very savage industry. She worked tirelessly, she had vision, strong intent, a willingness to learn, she knew a lot of powerful people in the industry, she went up for every part and she never gave in. In short she tried everything, but still to no avail. Like many other successful people (before they made it), she became exasperated; 'What else (she thought) am I supposed to do?' Then one day, after a particularly dry period without even the hint of ascent – no exciting work forthcoming and no potential for progress on the horizon (a point, in fact, where she felt like giving up) – she secured a part in a new TV drama (that she did not think she would get) and 'bang!', her entire existence changed in an instant. Everything happened at once. She said it was like leaning on a Chinese panel and falling into a different world. She was suddenly inundated with work, became pretty much a national idol and was being wined and dined by the kings and queens of show business.

What I have learned about success (and it was underlined in this article) is that it might take decades before you lean on that Chinese panel, or it might happen with the very next phone call you take. You never quite know. No one does. All they (I) do know is that it can and it will happen, and often in an instant.

That is why, if you have a dream and it means everything to you, it is worth holding onto for a little bit longer, it is worth persevering for a bit more time, it is worth another day, another audition, another setback.

I don't know when your Chinese panel will appear but I do know that it will not materialise if you give up. You are unlikely to lean on it if you are not in the game.

All the books I have read, and all the successful people I have met (and this cross-references with my own experiences) concur on this one single point: it is all about tenacity! The ability to keep going no matter what. At times you might feel like a lost traveller stuck in a Dante poem, climbing Mount Purgatory, believing that the empyrean paradise is never going to appear. Then suddenly, from out of nowhere, the stairway of Saturn that leads to the Queen of Heaven appears before you and – hey, viola – it happens.

In other words, no one really knows the secret of success, but they do know that it exists, and that for the tenacious few the journey is real, and the traveller is you.

Chapter 7

God is a House

I came home the other day after a trying conversation with a family member. She was struggling with a difficult life situation and I was encouraging her to seek some means of invisible support.

Pray, mediate, talk to your higher self, go and see a priest, talk to a tree!

She scoffed.

She didn't believe in stuff like that, stuff that she could not see. Her world did not expand beyond the addictions that had held her captive for so long.

'If there is a God,' she demanded, 'show him to me.'

Of course I could no sooner show her the definitive God than I could show her the quantum galaxies that lay at the very foundation of the world around us. I could neither articulate God nor explain God in a way that she would understand, other than to say that He was all around us, beneath every turned stone and inside every split log.

It bothered me that she could not see (and, to be honest, that I could not articulate) that there is a lot more out there than meets the eye. Just because you cannot immediately see it does not mean it has no existence. And it also bothered me because I wanted to help her, but the help she required was, at that moment in time, beyond my scope (mostly because she did not really want help, or even – she felt – need help).

Her arrogance bothered me.

I have learned a lot in my forty-eight years on this spinning blue planet, enough to know that there is a higher power, and also enough to know that the articulation of this divinity is galaxies beyond my understanding, let alone my vocabulary. All I do know is that it is there, it is benevolent and I can access it whenever I want to.

I wondered why she could not understand. I wondered why she could not see. And my wondering was becoming a noxious fog that became one more thing that bothered me. So I meditated on my wonderings and I looked for a sign that might cut a clarity through the miasma of my thoughts.

When I got home and walked through the garden to my house it came to me. I was given a clue. There were two ants on my garden path devouring a grain of sugar. They were completely unaware of my presence, or the fact that they were a size ten shoe away from total oblivion. I was way too big for them to see me. They would also, of course, have been completely unaware of the fact that they were – in our terms – only inches away from my house (which, if glimpsed for even a second, would have seemed to these tiny creatures like God Himself). My car, the road I lived in, the estate where my house was built, the city, the district, the country and the world, in fact, would have been way beyond their perspective. As far as these two ants were concerned their entire cosmos probably consisted of that piece of sugar and the 'vast and infinite' garden in front of my house.

Then I imagined these two ants talking to each other (as ants, I am sure, are prone to do), rather like I had just been talking to my family member. One of the ants was saying to the other, 'No I'm serious. I reckon there is a lot more out there than you and I can see – other creatures, other worlds. I bet there is a whole universe out there that we don't even know about, things that we could not even begin to imagine.' (He was an articulate ant!) And the other ant, scoffing back arrogantly, mouth full of sugar, 'Oh yea! So show me! You and your fancy ideas. If there was more out there I am sure I'd know about it. Now be quiet and eat your dinner.'

The imagined vignette made me smile.

Just because the second ant cannot see the house does not mean that the house (the street, the city, the world) does not exist, and just because the first ant cannot articulate exactly what the house is, it does not mean that his belief in the house is folly.

Then I remembered my family member and our conversation – my evangelical zest, her pedestrian denial – and I imagined that, undoubtedly, all the while we spoke, we were being watched over by similarly large beings, equally astounded and amused by the arrogance and by the very small perspective.

Suddenly I understood.

In an instant I could see exactly why people do not, will not or cannot see. Many are small minded, more still are arrogant, and a plethora are simply too scared to imagine that they might be little more than ants in some random cosmic garden. And I also understood that I should not allow their lack of vision and their lack of belief (their understandable fear) to affect me.

I know the house is there, even if my understanding of it is not yet exact, even though my articulation of it is not yet fully formed.

The house is there and it is accessible, and that is all I need to know.

Chapter 8

A Garden Full of Bread

One of the best ways to understand life is to study nature. It holds all the answers if we take the time to surround ourselves by it and learn.

And you don't have to go far. I unearthed a diamond of information only the other day, and I didn't have to travel any farther than my back garden to find it.

Let me tell you how it went.

I was in my garden doing something I regularly do. I was giving. I often find that I receive my best lessons after I have first offered alms – in this case, bread. I was laying it out on the lawn for the birds. Within minutes (and with nothing more than half a loaf and a bit of stale teacake that I had snatched from Sharon) I filled the garden. As far as the birds were concerned there was abundance; you couldn't take a single step without hitting food. There was so much food that (I am sure) birds were migrating from across the globe for the feast. It was like Christmas time for the feathered flock. It was... well, there was a lot of bread. You get the picture.

Anyway, once the feast was spread I retired to my garden bench with a coffee and (teacake in hand, also snaffled from Sharon: toasted but not stale) I observed.

Literally, within a matter of seconds, three starlings landed in the middle of the garden, in the middle of the bread. I could see that two of the birds were very young and the third bird (obviously the mother) was feeding them from her beak. Suddenly, and without warning, the mother flew away. I could see (but the babies could not) that she had not flown far, just a hundred yards or so, onto a neighbour's roof, but patently far enough away for the chicks to feel abandoned. The two babies looked at each other helplessly, as though in an instant they had not only lost their mother, they had also lost their supply of food. I could see from their bewildered expressions ('Where the **** has mum gone?! Never mind Mum – what about our bread?!') that even though these two starlings were standing in the middle of a garden of bread, they could not see a single slice. As far as they were concerned there was absolutely no bread in the garden, even though they were actually standing right in the middle of all of it.

It was amazing. I loved it and I immediately related this incident to so many people I personally know who feel as though they have nothing, even though they are surrounded by abundant potential. They feel as though they are starving, yet there is available sustenance everywhere. They feel broke even though there is money growing on the trees. I, too, have often felt exactly the same way: trapped, hungry, in debt, not realising that the potential to be free, to eat and make money, was literally right under my nose.

At times we all feel as though we have no potential and that if someone is not feeding us bread from their beak, then there is no bread! What I have learned, and what I know, is this: we are all standing in a garden full of bread. If we can't see it, it is not because it is not there (we know it is there because so many other people are feeding themselves quite adequately), rather it is because we are not looking hard enough (or perhaps we are looking too hard!), we are too busy blaming others for our lack or we are waiting for others to feed us because – for one reason or another – we haven't learned to feed ourselves yet.

Back to the birds.

As I watched, I noticed that the baby starlings, getting hungrier by the minute and not quite sure where Mum was (or if she was ever going to come back), stopped looking for her to feed them, and started to forage around the floor themselves.

Well, as I am sure you can imagine, a bit of bread led to a bit of bread led to a bit more bread, and all of a sudden the starving infants were not only feeding themselves, they were actually satiated. And even though they perhaps thought their parent had abandoned them, she was actually watching from afar, aware that the long-term survival of her offspring depended not on her feeding them, but on them feeding themselves. The only way that was going to happen was if she stopped feeding them, forcing them to find their own sustenance.

And here endeth nature's lesson. When we take responsibility for our own nourishment, a piece of bread will lead to a piece of bread and success will lead to success will lead to even more success.

Eventually we realise that (if we look carefully enough) we are all actually standing on the very success we seek.

Chapter 9

Choose Life

The Buddha said that life is difficult. He recommended that we accept this as fact because by embracing difficulty we become comfortable with it, then and only then will the discomfort dissipate.

And yet all around us we witness people from all walks of life doing the mirror opposite, each searching (and prepared to pay handsomely for) the cure-all to life's ills: junk TV, fast food, fast cars, fast drugs and faster fame. Others, cornered and terrified by their own suffering, choose the ultimate panacea – suicide. There are even websites set up to celebrate the trend, giving instructions on the best ways to swap the incarnate for the ethereal, even proffering friends to share the journey (like some hideous coach trip). Some people of late have even suggested that this method of do-it-yourself departure is brave!

Lost (maybe), very sad (certainly), mentally unhinged (probably), you could also argue that suicide is a very selfish act. But brave?!

Several of my friends have brought a premature and violent stop to their earthly sojourn: one, using a length of rope strung from a garage beam; another, over a long period of time with cheap sherry; a third, with a cocktail of illegal drugs and a farewell note that left confusion and pain in its wake.

I mourn them all and I judge them not, but I have to tell you that when the bad news arrived my first thought was not that they were brave. To badge a suicide with the label of courage is perhaps to add license and purpose to its employ. It'd probably even act as an advertising banner for the vulnerable, the easily led and the want-to-be-convinced. Suffering scalds people, and suicide is oft used as a desperate balm. But should we really label this act courageous and its advocates fearless?

From my own experience of life, as a man who has been around a few corners and glanced, more than once (however fleetingly), at my own mortality (violence, illness, deep depression), the word 'fearless' does not really exist, only an understanding of and mastery over the biological processes of anxiety, adrenalin and depression. And the word 'courage' is certainly not used for those who choose an early exit at their own hand, rather it is reserved for those who join the poet Rumi's army of night travellers and go out into the dark to hunt down their fears.

Courage, after all, is not the absence of fear, but the fact that we act in spite of it. People, it would appear, see suffering as the anathema and medication and evasion as its cure. Certainly there are times when you hit such a low point that all you can do is medicate and evade. For some, it is a survival imperative, but in the long-term, certainly from my experience (and I have had a life-time of marinating in the sediment of discomfort), I have found the opposite to be true. It is by engaging our fears, facing our depressions and leaning into life's sharp edges that we are able to free ourselves from suffering's clutches. This is where valour lies. This is where courage can flex its muscles and strengthen its sinews. And it can be very intoxicating. I love the idea of using the discomfort of life as a vehicle for self-control and ultimately freedom. I have found great wisdom in my own suffering; it is the body's way of letting us know that something is amiss. It might be telling us that we are in the wrong job, the wrong relationship or the wrong life. It might be simply letting us know that we are pushing too hard or perhaps not pushing hard enough. Often our suffering is simply the pain of death and rebirth as we exit the spent reality that we currently inhabit – a job, a relationship, a town, a country, a paradigm. We are reborn through the womb of pain that separates the old life from the new reality we wish to join. When leaving one reality for another we experience a death and a birth, both of which are associated with pain. Understanding this can really help us to cope when pain knocks our door dressed as the bailiff of change.

Whatever the cause, I have found that if we are prepared to turn towards suffering and take an honest and sober inventory of our life, suffering can become a liberating force. Folk (myself included) are guilty of running to escape their pain when often the exit they require is in the very pain they flee. All growth takes place in the crucible of discomfort – if you are prepared to stay there for long enough.

If we truly wish to be warriors we need to step up and take on the bigger challenges, the most immediate of which exist in the present moment. The battles of yesteryear are ancient history and future shadows have no existence outside of unschooled imagination. And for those struggling with present demons, the hereafter probably holds less terror than the here-and-now, so they choose death as their repair because death is the lesser nemesis. I do not doubt that it takes courage to end your own life. Death is seen as the ultimate unknown. But is it a lesser courage than that which is needed to live on when one's life feels like needless torture? This reality, after all, is just as uncertain and just as unknown and the one we embrace in death.

And if ending this incarnation feels easier than living it out, then I am with the Buddha who said that life is difficult and that only by embracing difficulty will we find true enlightenment.

So, with this in mind, I say that when life offers you choice why not be really brave, be a warrior, step up. And ask for help if you need it, it is always there. Take medication if that is the temporary crutch you require, go to counselling, run a marathon if it helps, but please, please, please – choose life.

Chapter 10

Circle in the Sand

I read an interesting story the other day about a tribe in Europe called the Yezidis. Like many ancient peoples their world is one of superstition and ritual. Whilst most people find it easy to judge their beliefs as backward and primitive, I don't, because I look around me and see so many contemporary parallels. One such superstition practised by the Yezidis is the circle in the sand. When I read about the theory and practice of what amounts to a prison without walls or doors I was intrigued, excited, and to be honest, a little scared. I was intrigued because of the startling parallels; excited because a plethora of these imprisoning circles suddenly became visible in my own life (where before they existed as invisible and unexplained blocks). And I was scared because now that the circles had made themselves known I felt compelled to do something about them.

Let me explain more about how the circle works, and how it relates to us.

In Yezidi tradition, if someone, for whatever reason (usually malicious), draws a circle in sand around you, due to innate fears, ancient beliefs and superstitions it becomes impossible to escape, unless someone on the outside breaks the circle and lets you free. This belief is so ingrained, so powerful, that a member of the Yezidi tribe would eventually die in the circle if someone on the outside did not break it. It is as though an invisible energy field surrounds the person on the inside, leaving them trapped, forever at the mercy of those on the outside. You'd think, logically, that the trapped person would simply walk through the circle drawn in the sand and laugh at the mere notion that he was captive. The opposite is true. His belief in the circular gaol is so powerful that escape becomes impossible. There have been many documented cases of people dragging a trapped Yezidi forcefully from the unbroken circle (the belief is so ingrained that it is as if they are held there by some superhuman power, and one very strong man would not be capable of removing even a slight female or a child without first breaking the circle) only to find that the said Yezidi fell immediately into a deep trance that they did not exit until they were placed back in the circle. Only when the circle is broken from the outside can the Yezidi escape. As I said, it is easy to think this childishly primitive, even though for the tribe that is steeped in superstition it is as real as gravity. But when we look at our own lives, at our own society and its rules and regulations (should I say, superstitions), we see parallels that are startlingly similar. I have seen many friends become seriously ill with stress and depression when trying to break the circle of their social norm. As a young man my circle in the sand was the factory (which was actually more of an inherited identity than a job). I wanted to leave it, I was desperate to leave it, but try as I might I could find no escape. Every time I tried to break the barrier that circumvented my reality, I was frozen with fear until I took myself back into the safe zone where I quickly returned to my unhappy (but comfortable) norm. I was in a miserable marriage where I felt limited and unfulfilled. But there was a circle drawn in the sand around the union that I could not break. Every time I tried to leave the marriage terror struck, and I found myself gratefully going back to what was hated, but what was familiar. Similarly, when I desperately wanted to become a writer, the circle that surrounded my non-writer self would not allow me an exit. Like most people, I was waiting for someone on the outside to create a break in the circle to set me free, but that was a bit like waiting for a lottery win. When we rely on external forces to change our destiny we give over all our power to those outside influences. Like the Fates, they might help, but mostly they will not.

I was partly kept in the circle by my own hand (we often draw our own circle of limitation) and partly by my friends and relatives and social norms, all of which were very quick to scare me back into the circle should I try to escape. (Not always maliciously: people react to what they know, and what they know is usually limited by their own influences, their own upbringing and their inherited genes.) I started to look at the people around me (my friends, family and students), and I asked myself two things and tried to be as honest as I could in answering. Was I allowing them to draw circles in the sand around me? Often we do not grow because those closest to us advise us not to – perhaps telling us that where we want to go is the wrong path – and because we love them we trust their advice. Or perhaps we allow them to draw circles in the sand around us because we fear our own massive potential; we fear that our rate of growth might leave them disorientated, hurt, lost or even left behind. The second question was harder: Have I been guilty of drawing circles in the sand around the people I love? Are they limited because my fear of their growth is represented by the circle in the sand around them? Once we can answer these questions honestly, we can start to work on breaking the circle from the inside and making a run for freedom. This works for us, for those who imprison us and for those who we imprison. When you set them free you also set yourself free, and when you set yourself free, everyone in your world gets a taste of liberation. Your success is everyone's success, and everyone's success is yours.

Obviously, later when I became sick and tired of my very small reality and decided to challenge it for one that was a better fit, I did break my circle from the inside, and whilst it was very disorienting at first (terrifying at times), I soon got used to it (to the point that I started to break other imposed and self-imposed circles, entering and exiting realities almost at will).

This is hard stuff to get your head around, harder still to make the changes that need to be made, but then we were never meant to be in the game of easy. There is no growth in easy. Only when you break the Yezidi circle of your own free will do you truly own the will to be free.

Chapter 11

Counting Sheep

I am out on a three-mile run (to be followed by a session on the weights). I have been out every day, every week, every month, every year for the last thirty-five. Without fail, I am out. Summer, winter, high days and holidays. Even Christmas day has become a ritual of a run, followed by shower followed by a hearty Christmas-day breakfast. There are no seasons with my training because seasons are for the sheep. I do not stop training because of harsh weather. If it is pissing down, I am out; if it is feet-deep snow, I am out. If the weather is (mad-dog-and-Englishman) hot, I am out. Weather for me is just wallpaper. I am a serious trainer and I do not stop for anything, certainly not for the weather.

I am not long into the winter air before I spy my first sheep: a young guy at the bus stop smoking his lungs black and muckying my air. I look at him as I pass and think 'sheep'. It says 'smoking kills' on the cigarette packet, but he is tarring his lungs cancerous anyway.

I pass the newsagents and spy another sheep, buying the top-shelf porn while his wife struggles at the counter to pay the bottom-line bills. Loss-leader entry. Hard addiction as a by-product. An easy lure for sheep.

I pass a couple of greedy gluts farther along; they are waddling into the take-away for more food then either of them has earned, their veins furring up with every bite. I shake my head and think 'sheep, sheep, sheep', and I run on, adding pace to my step as though their cloy might be infectious and I need great distance to keep me in cure.

Before I have added a half mile to my run, a notorious gangster (of the local variety) passes me in his luxurious 4 x 4 (with obligatory blacked-out windows), the rotting fruit of his criminal labour: sheep! Fat, violent, criminal sheep. I can't help myself. It is what I see. So I run on, faster still. I need to be away from the darker orbits. They suck you in if you get too close.

Breathing hard, pushing my limits, I hit the hill part of the run (and I do love the hills). But I am stopped halfway up by an old school friend, half-pissed, high as Everest, teeth black with rot, some missing (knocked out because of his violent nature), pupils as big as black holes: a forty-seven year old with the body of a pensioner. An aspirant who became a sheep.

This is a hard run. The air is very mucky tonight.

I stop briefly, share a few pleasantries (things you say when you don't really have things to say), then I run on, away from my past, away from my dark potentials, away from another sheep. And I feel glad that I am out and running and feeling grand and residing in a body that can still earn me dollar, a body that would not look out of place on a young athlete. I feel quietly proud of myself for making the right choices and for making a silk-purse existence out of what could have been a sow's-ear life.

At home I gander at my reflection in the bathroom mirror. A sinewy, Marciano physique (functional, profitable) stares back. An athlete? Yes.

A lion? A leader? A master, perhaps?

No. Disappointed, I look in the mirror and my self-trained self-honesty smacks me right in the face. I see… another sheep.

A man with a mote in his eye like a factory girder.

A man so busy marinating in his own pride and narcissism that he fails to see his own glutinous judgement. A man who just wasted a wonderful run picking holes in his own projections (all cleverly disguised as sheep). And I realised then that I had slipped again and my training needed to go up a level if I was ever to be the leader of self I have always wanted to be. It is not this body that needs a hardy trek, rather I need to take my mind out for a fast sprint, where the inclement weather, the hills and the pace are not wasted on judging other men (the obese, the pornographic, the criminal and the illicit). The air (I realised) will always be mucky when my mind is so full of judgement.

Luckily I do love myself so I did not make the second mistake of judging the man in the mirror. I just redirected him back to the centre. And I do go out every day, so tomorrow I will give myself another chance and try again; tomorrow I will run myself, as always, into the zone, but I will not – I WILL NOT – run others into the ground.

Chapter 12

Embrace the Black Child

I had a dream the other night that I wanted to share; I've been experiencing a lot of anxiety of late. We are making our first feature film (*Clubbed*) at the moment and lots of old fears (of failure and success, of being liked and disliked, accepted, rejected and abandoned) have been coming to visit, and I was desperately looking for a metaphor that might help me deal with them before they deal with me. The anxiety was such that I was starting to think, 'Maybe the film world is not for me. Maybe I'm just not cut out for it. Maybe I should just up-sticks, buy a tea shop by the sea, while away my hours and end this mad dance I am doing with anxiety.' The feeling I was experiencing (to be honest) is no different to that which I've been feeling all my life. This one was just wearing a different hat, and the disguise fooled me there for a while. Anyway, I went to bed on a blanket of anxiety and asked God to give me some inspiration, a metaphor or at the very least a little direction.

The dream I was delivered did the trick. Let me share it with you.

I was at the side of the road and I noticed a beautiful black child in the gutter crying. The child was naked and covered in oil, he was terrified and snotty and dirty and – even though he was holding out his arms for comfort and solace (from anyone) – everyone, irrespective or race, colour or denomination was walking around and past him as though their compassion for the child's predicament was being swallowed by their fear of his condition. Even I felt an undefined repulsion and recoiled when he looked in my direction. I was reluctant to embrace him, perhaps worried that his fear was contagious. As the child approached me, arms out, a small quiet voice in the back of my mind whispered, 'Embrace the black child.' Never one to turn away from a Samaritan act, I followed the instruction, walked over to the child and put my arms around him. I not only embraced him, I completely embraced him, tightly, with love and with no judgement. The moment I hugged him he stopped crying and my repulsion dissipated to be replaced by the warm glow of love and peace. Then something else amazing happened; the child in my arms became sand, slipped through my embrace and blew away. That small quiet voice spoke the same words to me again, adding only a comma, a small pause between the last two words. It said, 'Embrace the black, child.'

Embrace the black! I understood.

So, when I woke up the next morning, the blanket of anxiety over my face, I did as I was bid and I embraced the black. I dove head first into my fear and marinated therein. Within seconds my anxiety had quieted, and the fear that had been feeding fat off my panic was suddenly, like the child in my dream, floating away.

What I took from my prophecy was not just that we should embrace our darkest, blackest fears in order to beat them (this is a belief that I have always had), what I also intuited was that the fear we often see as *out there*, is actually not. It is *in here* – in you. The 'black' is a beautiful frightened child (or children) from your close or distant past that you carry around inside and that is always looking for transition. When we encounter a situation in life that invokes this terrified child, it is our chance to liberate it once and for all; not by forcing it back in and quickly racing away from the life situation that triggered it, but rather by embracing it, with love, and without repulsion or judgement. In so doing you lose your fear not by fighting and killing it, but by facing it and letting it go.

We as a species spend a lot of time and energy turning away from discomfort, believing that comfort resides somewhere in the other direction. The opposite (I have found) is true. We get past fear by going through fear, and the longer we leave it, the longer we put it off, the bigger and badder the fear seems to get as though it is forcing itself into our consciousness, so that eventually it will be heard and we will have to deal with it. And ultimately, there is no running away. We will perennially find ourselves facing the same situations again and again until we offer freedom to the fear we harbour by bringing courage to our confrontations.

This knowledge brings a whole new purpose to my life. My dream, my message, my God-given metaphor tells me something of vital importance; it tells me 'why' I am so driven to court failure by chasing success. It is not so that I can have a film on at the cinema, neither is it so I can add a few zeros to my bank balance. Both of these are worthy-enough goals, but on their own, neither is enough. I push the envelope, I place myself on the bleeding edge and I court discomfort because I know that it will force me to face my greatest dreads, and in doing so will release my blackest fears. It is only in releasing our fears that we can live life the way it is mean to be lived; FREE.

Chapter 13

Everything That Happens to Me is Great!

An acquaintance read my article, 'Everything That Happens to Me is Good' and gave me one of those patronising smiles.

He asked, 'What if your house burned down? Would that be good?'

'Everything includes everything,' I replied. 'It is all-inclusive. It excludes nothing. If it did then it would not be (by its very nature) everything.'

He didn't understand.

'How (he asked) could everything that happens to you be good?'

He could see how some things that happen to me might be good, perhaps even many things that happen to me. But all things!?

I smiled (less patronisingly, more knowingly). He was obviously reading the words but not connecting with their meaning, certainly not on the right level of consciousness.

I said, 'Actually you're right. Everything that happens to me is not good… '

He smiled. See, he knew he was right…

'... everything that happens to me is great!'

If he was confused before, now he was head-shakingly perplexed.

I tried to explain to him that, if I allowed challenging life situations to determine my state of mind (to the negative), then my mood would always be at the mercy of chance. If, on the other hand, I practised the philosophy that everything that happens to me – no matter what – was the harbinger of knowledge and wisdom and growth, then my life would become a 24-hour day growing frenzy. It would be like living in a bag of fertilizer.

Life is a cyclical process of distillation. It is often only under extreme pressure that we truly boil away our impurities and clarity becomes evident.

Without pressure, diamond will stay coal, and without extreme heat, iron ore could not be layered into tempered blade. Fighting spirits are not developed outside of the arena, no matter how many times we try to convince ourselves that they are. When elite fighting corps want to develop warriors, they manufacture extreme life-threatening difficulties for their aspirants to face, because they know that there is no advance without adversity. And when the matriculating few don the winged beret, they do so with deserved pride because they know it has been earned.

When bodybuilders want to develop muscle, they head for the burn. The folk that develop the keenest physiques are the ones that get into the burn fast and stay in the burn long, and because they learn to associate the pain of the last rep with massive growth, they learn to look for the last rep, and they learn to love the pain.

Life offers us similar opportunities, if only we can see them as such (instead of whinging on about 'how hard life is').

If we can learn to see difficulty as opportunity then every difficulty will be welcomed. We will not only greet difficulty effusively, we will openly court difficulty; we will learn to love the burn that privation proffers, and marinate in the 'last-rep' pain of a life that always has, and always will be (as the Buddha said), difficult. Once we get this – once we really get this – the veil drops, the milieu transforms, we lean on that Chinese panel and 'bang!' The whole world changes and we truly can see that everything that happens to us is not only good, everything that happens to us is great.

Chapter 14

Fifty – Only Once

At an early stage of my development in all things internal, when I still prayed for luck if a good result was needed, and I still employed blame if things went awry, I was invited onto the 'Tom Robinson Radio Show' to talk about the release of my first book, *Watch My Back*. I hit it off with Tom instantly. He was generous with his time and kind with his advice; about my writing, my personal development and about life in general. I looked up to him because he had been (and still is) very successful, first as a pop singer and now as host of a popular Radio 4 show (*The Locker Room*). I remember at the time that I was desperately looking for (and not finding) an agent to represent my burgeoning literary talent. It is commonly acknowledged in the publishing world that securing an agent is as hard as landing an actual publisher (or as hard as a big bag full of hard things). The competition to make it into print has always been fierce, especially now, in the days when fame is seen as the panacea of a dissatisfied populace, and writing is often viewed as an easy entry into the pantheons of celebrity. As I said, it was an early stage of my development as a self-realised person and as a writer, and no matter how hard I tried I seemed unable to find an agent that would read my work, let alone offer to represent me. So I did what most people do in these situations, I started to tilt lances at windmills and blame all and sundry for my lack of success. It was (my chippy-shouldered ego informed me) because I was working class, it was because my book was a one-hit-wonder, it was because people 'didn't get me'.

There were a lot of becauses.

Feeling a little sorry for myself (if all else fails self-pity is as good a reward as a cream cake), I complained to Tom that, 'I can't get an agent. I really want one but no one's interested.' Tom looked at me, unable to stop his eyebrows rising into a question mark.

He said, 'How many agents have you tried Geoff?'

I said (quick as a flash), 'Oh, loads.'

I'd sent a flurry of emails and letters out in a day of mad exuberance, but never really bothered to follow any of them up.

Tom said (and this has stayed with me ever since. In fact, every time I feel as though things are not happening for me I remember his advice), 'Geoff, if there are fifty agents in London and you have only tried forty-nine of them, then you haven't done your job. If there are fifty agents in London and you have tried them all, but only once, then you still haven't done your job because second-time around you will be talking to different people on a different day, and they will have different needs and different moods. If you haven't got an agent, it is because you don't want an agent.'

Tom was telling me something that deep down I already secretly knew but perhaps did not want to acknowledge: if you really, truly want something you will move heaven and earth and all in-between to get it.

I use this advice now every time a goal seems illusive, or every time I hit a rock or a hard place (or I find myself betwixt the two), or every time I have tried forty-nine out of fifty, or fifty only once. I remind myself that when my desire is absolute, my want will become my intent, and it is entirely the job of intent to deliver reward.

Chapter 15
Gravity

I want you to try something for me next time you are in the bath (no, not that – you know what happened last time you tried that). As you exit and pull the plug, I want you to try a little experiment. As the water starts to empty, hold the plug just above the plug-hole.

I'll tell you what you'll feel: gravity!

It's gravity caused by the water being sucked (by the earth's gravity) into the hole. And as you hold the plug closer to the hole, the pull will get stronger and stronger; in fact, it will get so powerful that the plug will start to shake violently in your hand as it is urged in the direction of the flow. But – and this is the second part of the experiment – you will also notice that when you move the plug away from the hole, the pull (or gravity) will get weaker and weaker, until you reach a point just outside the orbit of the plug-hole where there is no gravitational pull at all, certainly not enough so as you'd notice.

Outside of the orbit you can observe the gravitational pull, but not be of the gravitational pull.

Exciting stuff!

You don't think so?

Let me tell you why it is so exciting to me. It is exciting because everyone and everything is a plug-hole. Or, to be more succinct (and less offensive), everyone and everything has a gravitational pull, and like the plug-hole we will be sucked in if we allow ourselves to slip too deeply into its orbit.

If you love your food, you will notice that food – especially of the junk variety – has its own gravitational field. We think about food, or we see food , or smell food, and miraculously we are sucked into its orbit and suddenly we find ourselves sitting at Greggs necking a party-pasty and a cream-cake dessert that we might as well paste right onto our bellies. Similarly, the salacious nature of porn in all its forms sucks us in (forgive the unintentional pun) like a planet into a black hole. We get a hint of bare ankle or a whiff of easy fortune and bang! We find ourselves in a gravitational field so strong that it pulls us into a wank-fest of imagined excess.

These are just two examples. We only need to look at the fact that, for instance, sexual pornography is a multi-billion pound industry to recognise what a powerfully global gravity it can have. It pulls in sheep by the billion! Power (or the desire for power) also exhibits a monumental, often destructive lure, as does any orbit that offers easy access as a loss-leader, and mass-addiction as a by-product.

These major, visible orbits are obvious enough, and like the plug-hole they are only really dangerous if we enter with ignorance or unschooled minds. The practised warrior does neither. He understands enough about gravity and orbits to stay on the periphery of the most treacherous, and only then enters on-guard or for specific purpose (but that is a different article). One might assume that the most obvious auras are the most dangerous orbits to enter. Not necessarily true. It is (I find) the more insidious orbits that we do not necessarily recognise as maleficent that often proffer the most peril. Like the devil, these orbits never do so much damage as when they convince people that they do not exist.

I am talking, of course, about the imperceptible orbits of other people – especially those whose strong charisma is coupled by a dark or ignorant intent.

We are surrounded on a daily basis by people who suck us into their orbit (deliberately or by mistake), and influence us in a very wrong direction. If you sit in the company of the critical and the cynical, it will not be long before your world view starts to reflect their twisted rhetoric. Have a regular beer with the criminal and the violent and I guarantee that within a very short period you will start to grow bulbous knuckles and apish arms. And we all know how quickly titillation in any subject can quickly metamorphose into reality itself. I have met many people who have gone from flirtatious magazine erotica to full-out, in-the-trap swinging, and somewhere along the way lost not only their integrity (often their marriages) but also their raison d'être. What is interesting with these types is the fact that their going astray is often profound, yet they still violently deny being lost at all.

But it is not all bad news. The dark is always juxtaposed by light. Where murky orbits can influence along the wrong path, bright orbits can influence us along the road to salvation. Slip into the orbit of a good motivational speaker, or a spiritual guru or a man of integrity and you will find a gravity that pulls you in all the right directions. Watch a film about Gandhi or Martin Luther King and you may be inspired to change the world. Read a book by Lance Armstrong and his gravity will be so strong that you will know categorically, one hundred per cent, that a return to good health is not a lottery but a choice. And if everyone has gravity, and gravity is what attracts things and people (and with them gifts), then why not make your own gravitational field so awesomely attractive that you pull nothing less than positive abundance into your universe.

I could say more on the latter, and I will… but on another day, in another article (I promise).

So, to conclude; know that everything has an orbit, know that everything has gravity and know that whilst you do get to choose which ones you enter, you may not always get to choose the ones you leave. So, be diligent, please. Some orbits are less forgiving than others, and once they suck you in they might not let you out again. I have stopped counting the friends I have lost because they chose the wrong orbit, or flirted with a gravity that was beyond their game. And once you are down that plug-hole, let me tell you, you ain't ever coming back.

Chapter 16

Having it Outside the Chippy With God

A man once spent an hour bragging to me of his fighting prowess, how he held an eighth dan in karate, a sixth dan in ju-jitsu and a fourth dan in some other exotic style of martial art that I had never heard of. He had the trophies on every shelf, lapels lined with worthy medals, and belts (of the black variety), well, he had them hanging from every pair of gi pants he owned.

I have many times found myself in such company, listening to tall-tale telling (how fast their style is, how technical, how awesomely powerful) and hearing of 'unique fighting systems' and 'devastating new styles' which (invariably) are hailed as the only 'real' art, with the added assumption (or should I say accusation) that everyone else (but them) has got it wrong – oh, so wrong.

Invariably, after suffering a short assault, I find myself thinking, 'Yes, you've got the paperwork, but can you have a fight? Outside the chip shop on a weekend, can you have it? Can you take what you have learned in the controlled arena and make it work for you in real life?'

They know the talk, the jargon, and they can demonstrate the demonstration, but none of it means shit if you can't make it work outside the chippy on a Friday night.

Now I am not the highest-ranking martial artist in the world, and I have no doubt that there are people out there right now that could talk me under the table when it comes to technique and lineage. But let me tell you, when it comes to real combat I have been around a few corners. And the things I have learned from my very rich experience I can definitely and categorically make work for me against the Neanderthal that wants to try and flatten the world with my head (if not all of the time, certainly the majority of the time).

The late (great) Bruce Lee felt that many arts had become so 'crammed and distorted' by their own dogma, so self-important about their superiority over other arts, so caught up with their own classical mess that they had forgotten their purpose. People focussed so much on demonstrating the superiority of their art over others that their art became superior to others, but only in demonstration.

Everything comes through the physical. No one gets to peak Everest without first going through base camp. So, if the art is authentic, it will bring its practitioners higher consciousness, but only through harder contact. If the art is synthetic, then higher consciousness will be replaced by higher ego, developed through hardly any contact at all.

Certainly not any contact with reality.

Knowing twenty systems and taking weekend courses with popular gurus does not a warrior make.

You can always tell warriors. They don't reveal themselves in what they say, but in how they live.

Being a pragmatist I notice these things.

And lately I have noticed it again. This time in the world of spirituality.

It would seem that a new classical mess has been born.

I recently listened to a podcast conversation between two of the world's top spiritual gurus. Two men that, actually, I greatly admire. They were talking about the nature of consciousness and God and the spiritual development of the species throughout the ages. The conversation was esoteric but quite nice. In fact, these two men were wonderful together, mutually appreciative and obviously very well-versed in all things celestial. They talked about (and complimented) each other's work, what they disliked about the work of other people whose work contradicted their own and how they found it difficult to comprehend why many so-called learned men and women had apparently learned so little.

I can't say that I understood everything they said, because much of their dialogue was in the language of eastern religion, the language of academia or simply the language of their own categorised school of thought. But what I did understand and what I did ken (and what caused me to abort the listening early) was this; these two spiritual behemoths talked an awful lot about the superiority of their own development (or the development of their system) and an awful lot more about how underdeveloped so many other systems were. They talked very little about God, or about how to make God a practical part of your everyday life. They also delighted in being acknowledged by one half of the current crop of flavour-of-the-month gurus whilst simultaneously being angered at the criticism accorded them by the other half.

I was only five minutes into the conversation when I started to get that uncomfortable feeling in my gut (isn't there an important chakra there somewhere?) that told me I was back in familiar territory, that I had heard all of this before, in the higher (middle and lower) echelons of martial arts. Perhaps I had already learned all I needed to learn from these two lovely, learned characters. It was right back to belts and grades and accolades and… well, you know the story. So I wondered if (actually, I was sure that) I was listening to the wrong people. I mean, do we really care and do we really need to care about names and labels, about grades and accolades, about being recognised or about being dismissed?

I only ask this because I have often found myself chasing similar impostors, only to be disappointed when below the facade of gold feet, I found brass.

I do not claim to be free from ego (this article would not exist if there was no ego), and certainly I am no expert in technical and terminological religious dogma, but let me tell you, when it comes to the life lived, I have some time behind the wheel. And the things that I have learned from my very rich experience I can definitely and categorically make work for me when I am at my weakest and need to be at my strongest.

So when the conversation becomes foreign with terminology and the words are religiously verbose and the teachers don their parade medals, I neither spin nor toil, because whilst I certainly do not understand enough, I understand enough to feel God. In that place of feeling, the world of academe, and the world of honours and acknowledgment, shrinks into insignificance.

I am not the highest-ranking spiritual aspirant in the world, and I have no doubt that there are people out there right now that could talk me under the table when it comes to the technical and the academic. But let me repeat, when it comes to the grist, I have felt God. *I have felt Him.* And the things that I learned from my moments of clarity I can definitely and categorically make work for me outside the chip shop of life, if not all of the time, certainly most of the time.

Chapter 17

Hypocrite

I am going to make this article short and succinct. My reasons for doing this amount to two: 1) I am halfway through a training session and I don't like to interrupt my training, not for anything (not even for a buttered tea cake or spontaneous sex… well, maybe a buttered tea cake!); 2) The nature of this article is… uncomfortable.

As you are all probably aware by now, I like being uncomfortable. I like the ache of growth. As Ken Wilber once said to a young aspirant (a friend of mine called Richard Munn) who was suffering not a little discomfort, 'You are sitting on a gold mine of pain.'

I digress. So, with both points in mind, I'll cut right to my quick; I am a hypocrite.

No chicanery, no riddles, no tricks or excuses, just a simple solitary fact. Many of the things I teach

– abstinence, self-control, non-judgement, etc. – I either struggle with or I fail at on a regular basis. My wife knows it, my children know it, my friends secretly know it, my students (I am sure) know it (they should – I tell them often enough!) and, of course, I know it.

They all know it, but interestingly they all still love me very dearly, despite my shortfalls (or perhaps because of them).

The reason I am telling you is threefold; I am embarrassed by it (when you are a teacher you should always try to be what you teach), I am blackmailed by it (my inner opponent is always threatening to out me) and I am massively excited by it.

It is the latter part of this triumvirate that I want to talk about.

The excitement.

I look at my life, I look at my wife and children, I look at my job, and I look at me and I am extremely happy. I love my life. I love being who I am. I even love (and am greatly amused by) other people's mistaken perception of who I am: the toughest man in Britain (please! I'm not the toughest man in my house), fearless (the opposite, in fact, is true. It is only my acute state of fear that enables me to be so prolific), a liar (people who read *Watch My Back*, often even people who feature in the book, think it is a bunch of lies – especially those who stepped violently into my world and had to be carried back out again) and a fake (more than once I have been accused of buying my martial-arts grades). Granted, my multiple instructorships do seem out of context with the norm, but I have never been one for the norm, and believe me, when you are training three times a day with some of the best people on this spinning planet, dan grades become so easy to attain that in the end they are hardly worth talking about or having. Let's be frank here. It is very hard for me to take criticism from people who do not even meet their own standards.

Back to the excitement!

I am greatly encouraged by a life that allows me to be successful, even when I make mistakes. Here is a universe that does not demand perfection of its winners, only undying persistence. I gave up conventional work fifteen years ago and vowed only to do the things that I truly love doing for the rest of my life. And I have stuck with that. My job is writing about things I love. I teach martial arts and personal transformation (which I love). I wake in the morning and I love my life. I go to bed in the evening and always say to Sharon, 'What a great life we've got.' (And she always agrees. Well, she did get to marry me and I am – she assures me – a bit of a catch.) I look at the children we have produced and they make me proud. I look at the friends I have made and feel grateful. I look at the volume of work I have produced and I feel inspired. For a kid who was told to stick to a factory job and not to 'get above your station', I am ecstatic at the way my life is unfolding. And this is the good bit; it is not unfolding in this way on its own. It is unfolding beautifully because I take on difficult tasks, I lean into the sharp edges and I embrace the uncertainly and ambiguity of life. In fact, I have a highly-developed tolerance for both ambiguity and uncertainty. And this, my friends, is where the kernel of my excitement lies. If I can live an amazing life, the life of my dreams, even though I still make mistakes and even though I often fall, imagine what it is going to be like when I stop being such a hypocrite and start getting it right (if not all of the time, at least most of the time).

Imagine what your life will be like when you do the same, you bunch of hypocrites!

It will be the life of mass abundance that is promised in every Bible and prophesised on every philosophical tablet.

So now when the guilt kicks in, the embarrassment at failing (again) rises, and the inner blackmailer starts getting loquacious, I remind myself that whilst I am not getting it right all of the time, I am getting it right enough of the time to make my once substandard life quite amazing. And whilst I do definitely fall, I do – definitively – never give up. Let me say that again because it is what my success pivots on: I never give up! I step away sometimes to take respite, I fall often and have to seek Invisible Support to find my feet, and I reflect and renew my purpose (often on a daily basis) but I never give up. For every seven times I get knocked down, I get up eight. And when I do get knocked over, I never blame. I leave the blame for the powerless. Like the master archer who misses the target, I always come back to myself for the source of error.

You don't have to win all of the time to be a success (I do what I can and allow God to do what I can't). Just be tenacious and success will stick to you like a fat kid's school shirt.

So, with that in mind, I will echo the words of the great motivational guru, Zig Ziggler: 'Listen to everything I say, but do not look at me too closely. I am still working on this stuff myself.'

Chapter 18

Reservoirs of Pain

The pain of countless dark episodes fills my chest, the world around me forms a miasmatic cloud, feelings threaten to implode or burst out in violence and… I thank God for the abundance of energy! I filter it through my quill and bleed nectar onto the page.

Memories of childhood abuse rampage through my veins. The trigger might be a name overheard in a conversation, an article in the paper or the smell of old factory. My body trembles at the assault as rapine thoughts colonise me and… I thank God for the plenty because the throb of my terror is malleable and I make it into a Roman script fit for Oscar.

The angst born of 10,000 rejections sets up camp in my dizzy belly until the dizzy turns terrible and the terrible screams from the inside of my skull, 'Run,

run, fucking run… ' To be honest, a small part of me *does* run – out of the seat and out of the building – but a Bigger Self stays. It steps up and… I thank God for my terror because I am making a courage-cake, and terror is the vital ingredient.

When the ache of loss trembles across my surface and my agony is leagues deep and profligate, I am again grateful to God because my reservoir of pain is the portal to a prolific life.

I am not successful despite my pain, I am successful because of it.

Whilst others may drown in their dark lake, I throw back a grateful pail and draw my fill.

Chapter 19
Jesus is a Factory Labourer

(Note: When we come to the part that says 'Jesus', please feel free to replace it with whatever name suits your conviction).

Jesus is a factory labourer! It's true; honestly, it came to me as a revelation halfway through my daily run.

Jesus... is a factory labourer.

Blasphemous? Maybe. I don't think so but... I'll take my chances.

God often talks to me mid-run, when my conscious filter is switched off and my internal dialogue is a simmering background noise. When He speaks I listen, and this time when He whispered gently into my heart He told me that Jesus of Nazareth, the Nazarene, the

Christos, God's son on earth, is pretty good with a brush and a shovel. I suppose I should explain.

I have a friend. I like this friend very much, and I love to chat with her. And of late she has taught me a great lesson (which I will get to).

She is a factory owner/ spiritual-aspirant and quite fancies herself as a bit of an all-round altruist. My friend also prides herself on her character because she is in favour with some weighty spiritual gurus and can parley on all things esoteric.

But here is the rub: whilst she is a great girl, her 'valleys and hills' are not yet levelled, because whilst her best game is sharp and inspirational, her worst game is dull and paltry. She treats those (she feels are) above her like sovereigns, but those who (she feels) are subordinate – her factory labourer, for instance – she treats like untouchables.

Why? Because she discriminates. Because she can!

But she shouldn't, because her labourer in the factory is Jesus.

When my friend is in my company she is regal, generous to a fault, funny, intelligent and gregarious. There is nothing she would not do for me.

But I know that she holds me in high regard, so it pays to don her best gown.

When this lady is with her guru she is the epitome of grace; grateful, courteous and complimentary in the extreme.

But her guru is her guru, and you can't let your mask slip when the master is in the house.

And when she is with customers in her factory she is the sham servitor extraordinaire.

But she is a savvy economist, she has read all the books and knows enough to know that the customer is (always) right, even when he isn't. It brings repeat business.

But, when it comes to her labourer, her best game is lacklustre, her grace is a disgrace and her economics become, well, uneconomical.

Why should she do any better? What profit is there in respecting the man with the brush and shovel?

Unfortunately, my friend just doesn't understand that... her labourer is Jesus Christ.

Her labourer is me.

Her labourer is her guru and her customer.

Actually, her labourer is the king, the queen and the common man.

In the Bible, Jesus says, 'How you treat the least of us is how you treat me.'

My lovely friend treats me, her guru and her customer royally, because she distinguishes us as different from her labourer, perhaps higher than her labourer, perhaps more worthy, so she brings out the best crockery and no request is too much trouble.

Who's going to notice the ill-treatment of one seemingly insignificant floor sweeper?

Actually, life notices. I notice. Her guru notices. And her customers, if not already, will eventually notice too. Because how you treat One is how you treat all.

The One wears many hats. She might be your wife or your mother, He might be your son or your husband, It might be your neighbour or your lover.

And Jesus, well, he passes through this way more often than you might imagine, looking for the humble, the aspirant and the cross-carrier. And when He arrives it is not announced with trumpet call and lines of hierarchy standing aside the carpet rolled and red.

That would be too obvious.

People would know. And in knowing, people would wear their best mask tight, they would doff their posh hat in low bow, and sparkle with their charity medals lined on lapel.

To sort the wheat from chaff, to repel the vainglorious sycophant and draw the genuine servitor, He usually prefers to take a more humble disguise (He certainly tends to arrive as someone difficult to like). Perhaps the Mighty will come as a whiffy down-and-out with begging fingers and a newspaper bed, or perhaps a dusty peasant riding into town on a donkey, or, if he really wants to be incognito, he might disguise himself as something startlingly routine like, oh, I don't know... a factory labourer, with shovel and broom perhaps?

Be well (but be observant).

Chapter 20

Metaphysical Self-defence

Metaphysical self-defence (MSD) advises us that we attract into our lives what we continually and emotively think about, especially when we experience fear (fear is the perfect example of emotive thinking). It's the law of attraction. So I have learned from concrete experience not to think about, talk about, imagine or ruminate on violence. Certainly I do not allow myself to fear violence, or I will definitely create it.

When I was thirty years old all I thought about was violence. I thought about it, talked about it, read about it, watched it on video and even dreamt about it. And all of my thinking was emotive (I even had a weapon in every room of my house, in case someone broke in and I needed an immediate appendage). So much so that my life became copiously savage. If violence was money I was a multi-millionaire.

Then one day it hit me. That eureka moment. I suddenly realised that the violence was not happening around me, it was happening through me. It was not occurring despite me, it was manifesting because of me. Excited (and for validation) I checked out the bibles of the world, looked at everything from motivational books about the power of thought, right through to *The Tibetan Book of the Dead* and Dante's *Divine Comedy* and...they all confirmed my belief: that what I thought about emotively I would create. I realised that I was and always had been a master thinker, without even knowing it. I had manifested into my life, through the sheer power of my thoughts, (literally) thousands of people who wanted to fight with me. Thousands. I created nightclubs, pubs, bars, road-rage incidents and arguments in restaurants and at work. I was literally surrounded by violence. I even manifested a huge fight at a friend's christening, because all I thought about was violence.

On realisation of this I became very excited.

Not because of the violence of course, rather by of the power of my thinking.

So I reversed my thinking. I stopped thinking, talking, watching and partaking in violence, I removed the weapons from every room, emptied my life of any reference, remembrance and residue of violence and I began thinking about what I did want to attract. I placed powerfully positive books in every room of my house, and started to think emotively about my dream life as a full time writer of books, plays, films, articles, newsletters – anything that entailed the written word with me as the man behind the quill. Soon it started to trickle in through the black hole of my imagination. Then the trickle became a steady flow, then the steady flow a gush and the gush and tsunami of books, plays - I was writing for five magazines and being asked to write films. Before very long my dream was a living reality. I had manifested it.

My new-found success did not happen by accident, it happened by design, it was not a stroke of luck it was a heavily planned campaign, nobody gifted it to me, I gifted it to myself with the power of my emotive thinking.

Now, if there is anything in my life that does not fit, I emotively re-tailor it with my thoughts, and if my life seems to be going off track, then I get myself back on line in the same way.

It is not the world out there that gets dark and light, it is our thoughts (in here), acting upon the world. So if you want to change the world, you only have to do one thing; change your thoughts.

Chapter 21

No Such Thing as a Locked Script

Fifteen years working on a script (or many versions of a script), a month away from principle photography (first day of filming), four weeks from finally taking a life-long project onto a five-week-shoot and the director wants me to do another draft?

'I think we can tighten it up a bit,' he says, nodding affirmatively and smiling.

'Actually, I think you can fuck off a bit!' I sub-vocalise.

I am sure he could see by my dumbfounded, defeated, can't go-there-again, hang-dog expression that I might not (probably didn't) have another 'polish' in me and that, actually, if he asked for one more draft, one more time, I might just have a boxing flashback and knock that nodding head off his shoulders.

I didn't do that, of course. I just smiled and said, 'OK, one more go.'

This was only my first feature film, and whilst I was still a relative neophyte in the industry I knew enough to understand the old adage that 'all writing is rewriting'. I had enough reference points from my varied background to understand that drilling and polishing is what separates the nearly-good from the really-good, and the really-good from those that consistently piss excellence.

So we got back to the grind and I silently dreamt that this draft might be the last draft that delivers me the screenwriter's nirvana, the 'locked script'. But alas, a week later we were on it again, and a week after that again, and then again. And then finally, on the very eve of the shoot, we made some more minor changes and the director asked the producer to send 'this one' out as the locked script, the shooting draft (the version from which the cast and crew work directly).

I breathed a deep sigh of relief and thought, 'Thank **ck for that.'

My relief (I have to admit) at finding the Holy Grail was arrogantly juxtaposed by the thought that 'all this rewriting and rewriting is so unnecessary.' And I have to also admit that I continued to harbour a wee small resentment because of it.

That is until principle photography, when I finally realised what it's all about.

Film is a serious business. Professional people were going spend a hefty chunk of their finite lives working night and day to make my words manifest. I was witness to 200 crew as they began in earnest the spend on a £2-million budget (raised independently through private investors: real people risking real money). And I have to tell you that I was overwhelmed with gratitude towards the director, Neil Thompson and the producer, Martin Carr (who ever-so-gently guided me through draft after draft) because I realised suddenly that there could be no worse feeling in the world than turning up on the first day of filming, seeing your work performed by professional actors and knowing in your heart that the script was one or two drafts premature (that we had pulled the apple from the tree before it was red and ripe).

I spent five blissful weeks on that shoot and there was not a single day, watching these amazing artisans lift my script onto a canvas of glossy celluloid, when I did not think, 'Thank God I did all those drafts. Thank God I polished and polished.' Because if I hadn't, let me tell you, it would have been a long, long shoot.

My second epiphany actually happened just as early as the first and proved even more instructive, nay profound. One of the lead actors approached me (script in hand, brow furrowed) a couple of days into the shoot and 'wondered' if I would mind him changing a 'small something' in his scene. His small something was a great insight. It made such a difference to the character he was playing and added a new dimension to the scene. I gratefully nodded my assent and said, 'Great idea. I love it.'

As he walked away it hit me again. Another eureka! It cracked me right across the swede.

There is no such thing as a locked script!

I realised in that very instant that for the next five weeks my script would, if it was any good, continue to evolve and change. Not only was this inevitable, it was also expected and very welcome: it meant that the script could and would and should get better and better. There is no locked script.

And even later still, in the editing suite, the shape would change yet again when the rushes (the scenes we had shot) spoke to the editor and the director and asked, advised (sometimes demanded) that they should evolve.

I realised from this enlightening process that looking for a locked script is a danger to the art of making films. It is tantamount to rushing the process. So now when I am working on a film, no one has to ask me to do a rewrite. I am the first person there demanding (begging for) a read through (when the actors read the script to see if it plays), I am the one asking for a rewrite, a polish, looking for notes, criticism, critique, suggestions – anything that might help the script work better and get us closer, if not to a locked script, certainly to a script that is mature enough to honour a collaborating cast and crew, and ready for the editor to weave his magic in the post-production.

I have also allowed the concept of *no locked script* to spill into my other realities. I realised that my relationships are also works in progress. They should never be locked, and they will always need attention. My business regularly gets another draft because if it is not moving forward in this fast economic-river, then it is moving backwards and drowning. And my health and fitness must by necessity go through draft after draft, until time immemorial, because this incarnation is a film that will take a lifetime to wrap.

I intend to continue rewriting all aspects of my life, never again looking for the locked script, because not only does the locked script mean your works can no longer expand, but the very act of looking for it creates conflict and anxiety. The locked script you search for in earnest does not exist. There is no such thing as a locked script.

Chapter 22

The Hand of Experience

The other day I was asked if spiritual growth was possible without concurrent intellectual expansion. In other words, can you grow spiritually if you are not growing intellectually?

I personally love to study. I find it stimulating and inspiring to read about other people who have walked the path. As a teacher, I always encourage aspirants to read widely and to expand their understanding and their vocabulary. I think it is important as well as enjoyable. But ultimately, whilst I believe that expanding the intellect has many benefits, it is not an essential prerequisite to developing spirituality. Many people surmount great spiritual peaks through feeling and intuition alone. Most of the old shamans were not conventionally intellectual or well read (or even read at all). They could not quote Lau Tzu, or Goethe or Dante, but it did not stop them from connecting with and becoming great conduits for God.

If you are going to flex your intellectual muscles (and I recommend that you do) remember that for knowledge to be of any benefit at all it must be placed into the experiential world. Knowing is not the same as doing. And you only truly own what you have experienced. Everything else is just decoration. Until the point of practice, all knowledge remains impotent.

Having said that, one of the first things I do innately when I take on a group of people to teach is get them reading widely. I escalate the difficulty of the read, advising them to 'just read', even if initially they do not understand what they are ingesting. I do this as a matter of course. It is a compulsory element because I know that in the age of TV, DVDs and dumbed-down journalism, very few people read anymore, and when they do, they do not challenge themselves. This knowledge helps me when I am teaching. People primarily come to me because they are looking to escape dark realities (bad relationships, limiting beliefs, poor jobs, unfulfilling lives), and whilst I am practised at articulating how I found my way, there will always be a part of the aspirant that will want my words validated from other sources. So giving them books to read by other travellers helps people to trust what I offer.

Ultimately though, the words and the books are only there to encourage and catalyse personal experience, so that they can be the proof. Words without experience are ephemeral. What gives words life is action.

There is a danger of mistaking knowledge of the journey for the journey itself. If people are not careful they can get too caught up in intellectualisation. If it is not tempered in the forge of experience, knowledge can become a wank-fest of self-congratulatory narcissism. I have fallen into this trap myself, quoting the latest flavour-of-the-month guru to show my level of intellect. But I have also fallen into the trap of judging other people who I think might be guilty of over intellectualisation. When I was studying for a master's degree and had to read lots of verbose tomes, I really hated the language of academe because I felt that it was completely inaccessible to the man on the street. But to pass my degree I had to read it, and I also had to write it. And ultimately, I was glad I did, because it pushed me to expand, and enabled me to understand a language that was not open to me before. And that, of course, gave me immediate access to the writings of people I might once have failed to understand. So now I encourage other people to read books that are beyond their scope for the same reasons. The danger is (as I said) when the intellectuals intellectualise but never put the words into action. In the world of metamorphosis, action is all. And if the anti-intellectuals don't become more open-minded, they might miss out on something of real import.

I am aware that I have possibly offered you contradictory advice here, so in conclusion I'll tell you what my life has told me thus far and what is as real as gravity to me. Reading is great, writing is better. You discover things that you didn't know you knew when you write. But when it comes to the actual grist, experience is everything. When I am attracted by a speaker or a guru or a swami it is always because they have experienced life in all its wonder and awe. If you climb Everest or go to the moon or overcome a debilitating illness, people will cross the globe to share your orbit because everyone wants to touch the hand of experience.

And intellectuals? Well, some might say that they grow on the trees.

Chapter 23

The Harvest of Service

You know what I love, what makes me smile, what makes me laugh out loud? When you talk to people about service and they give you that patronising 'he's-a-bible-pusher' look. The reason it makes me smile is because people just miss the point. And in missing the point they miss the greatest opportunity that has ever been or ever will be presented to them – the opportunity to serve (and in serving, the opportunity to become the recipient of service). Because service is the secret to perpetual motion. It is an investment that always brings a healthy return. A deal that cannot fail.

I learned all about the power of service many years ago, after a midnight epiphany, which occurred following a long, hard year of stepping into my fears.

After my moment of clarity, I wrote a book called *The Formula*. It was not rocket science, and it was certainly nothing I had not read before in other places, but after my sudden union with God the knowledge was somehow more vibrant and real. I couldn't wait to tell people about it but of course the people I told looked at me like I was an alien that had just landed on their rhododendrons!

The message I received was that everything I gave out would return. The secret to perpetual motion is service.

You will probably have read this in other places. I know that the Buddhists talk about the reciprocal universe all the time, but as I said, this was different. This was no longer a piece of intellectual information. It was, to me, hard fact. When I cross-referenced the formula with my profligate backstory, the message was validated over and again. I was so excited. All I had to do to receive whatever I wanted was to serve. It works in every aspect of life, from business to relationships. It works on the internal microcosm and on the external macrocosm. Wealth, in all its disguises, was just an act of service away. What I also became acutely aware of was that even though I offered this message to everyone I met, especially to those I loved, it was only accepted by a small few. I realised quite quickly that the information would always be ephemeral to those who had not experienced it. All I could hope was that my words might inspire others to seek out the same experience and prove to themselves that service was always a highly profitable affair. It brings a better return than any commodity, and it never has a bad day on the stock market. It has helped me in every aspect of my life, to the point that I stopped looking for people I might profit from and started looking out for those I could serve. Especially difficult people. Because that is where the rich returns lie. As it says in the Bible, when you serve a prisoner, you serve God. So when someone came into my life who I was uncomfortable with (let's be honest, serving nice people is easy), someone who was difficult, especially someone I was repelled by, I tried my best to serve them.

Even if it was just with a kind thought or prayer.

The Buddhists call the latter Tonglen (the art of breathing in people's pain and breathing it back out again as love). It is really effective when I want to serve someone who does not want to be served. It allows me to help them from a distance. When my dad was dying I went to him most nights in my meditation and massaged him and told him I loved him. Being an old-fashioned gent, my dad would have been uncomfortable with this tactile approach in the flesh, but from afar he was very receptive to it. In fact, he told my mum one morning that I had been with him all night, and that he enjoyed my visit.

I hadn't been with him in person, but I did visit in my mediation.

As a man who has experienced the good and the bad (and the ugly) out there I can categorically tell you, without any doubt, that this is a reciprocal universe. And you can plug into it anytime you like. When I was unschooled in the art of reciprocation, I would allow my thoughts free reign and they brought me little joy and a lot of heartache. Now I take the helm, and I direct my thoughts, my words and my deeds to good. If I sit on the tube in London, I might tell a hundred people (in my head) that I love them. I have a cafe I love to visit in Leicester Square in London. I order a coffee and I sit watching thousands of beautiful people go by. As each one passes I say to them (again in my head), 'I love you. I love you', knowing that I am planting a harvest. Again, I would recommend that people, where they can, take on the bigger challenges. Those that they are most uncomfortable with are the ones that need your service first. If we are talking real power here, then service is the place to be. It is all-powerful, especially when that service involves the big stuff like forgiveness and non-judgement.

I also serve myself by tackling my addictions and working on all areas of my development. And I serve others by recognising that they are an extension of me, and me of them. And when people think I have gone all alien (and that I am trampling on their rhododendrons), I smile and smile and smile. Not only are they missing the chance to be a part of something amazingly powerful, they are missing out on the chance to connect to the greatest reservoir of gold in the known universe: service.

Chapter 24

The Jeremy Kyle Experience

Some people are successful and happy. Others are not. Why?

Why is it that some can turn a dark past into a bright present whilst others just end up getting head butted on *The Jeremy Kyle Show*?

My questions were triggered by a friend of mine, a fellow writer, who once accused me of being successful simply because I was lucky. His censure pissed me off. I was very angry, not least because luck is something you associate with gambling and I do not play the odds. I am a man who sits for thousands of hours at a computer and punches my lottery onto the screen.

Anyway, it was my anger that got me to thinking. Why is that two people from similar backgrounds, in an identical employ, end up on disparate rungs of the success ladder?

After a brief mentation I reached a conclusion of sorts, a philosophy, if you will. The only difference between me and my fellow scribe was not in the degree of luck we had each experienced, but in the breadth of our individual life perspectives. He charged his bad luck with impediment, I used every experience as grist. He saw the world as his nemesis, I viewed the whole universe as my fellow conspirator. His marriage breakdown, custody problems and health issues were recycled into worthy blames and justifiable causes for his paltry existence. My childhood sexual abuse, manic depression, acrimonious divorce (and a litany of betrayal, crime, violent death – lots of violent death – self-harm and illness) were rich veins that I cathartically bled onto the page.

We had both lived difficult, one might say dramatic lives, and whilst history demands precedence in our past, we do get to decide how we live our present.

While I chose to use my profligate backstory as a reservoir for ripe material, he chose the road of self-pity and blame.

And that is my philosophical gist. Choice!

I know it's not Goethe and it's certainly not Gurdjieff, but it keeps me in the game, it keeps me on the payroll and best of all it keeps me off *The Jeremy Kyle Show*.

Chapter 25

The Long Day

I am writing this article for a very selfish reason. In fact, I write all my articles and books and films and plays and journalism for a very selfish reason. Everything I write I need to read. So when I write it, it helps me, and I know that if I send it out into the ether, not only will it help everyone who reads it, eventually it will come back to me, I will re-read it, and it will help me again (because by then I may have forgotten the message).

I am prone to forget the message.

The message is about fear!

We all feel it, and every day that sees us spinning and toiling in resistance is a long day.

It is OK to feel scared. In fact, fear contains hidden benefits. So, if I have caught you mid-terror

– congratulations – you are probably on the cusp of a great discovery.

At the end of this piece I am going to ask you all for a huge favour. I hope you will oblige.

There is a lovely old Japanese metaphor about pain and fear and growth. I always recite it to myself when I am up against a wall of fear and easier options suddenly seem like my only escape. It goes something like, 'The iron ore feels itself needlessly tortured as it goes through the furnace. The tempered blade looks back and knows better'.

When my torture starts to feel needless, I remind myself of how many times I have been through this fire and how true it is: that you do always look back afterwards, and you do always know better.

Iron ore and tempered blades! Inspiring words. But without action they remain just that. Words, with no power.

It took me many years of experience (in the forge) before I truly understood this. Words do not transform us; massive action transforms us.

But words can inspire us to action. And words can weaken fear and better enable us to break free from its bonds – especially when those words have been tempered by experience. One of the greatest things I learned was from a man of experience who taught me my most valuable lesson: everyone feels fear! It's not just me. This one tutorial above all others inspired me to act. I realised that I was not a coward, that everyone was scared, and it changed my life.

One of the most debilitating aspects of fear is the false belief that we are not only its victim, we are its *only* victim (and for some reason the spiteful universe has decided to give us more than our fair share). I always felt this way as a younger man. But I was wrong. I was not alone. And if I was getting more than my fair share it was not because some Higher Power had it in for me, quite the opposite in fact. The reason I enjoy such a prolific life now is not despite fear, rather it is because I have become an alchemist, transforming the molten ore of fearful existence into the tempered blade of a golden life.

There are many ways to beat fear. There are a plethora of methods that can hold it at bay, even help you to understand it. The better player actually befriends fear. The aspirant uses it as fuel, the master rises to a level of consciousness where it does not exist because its fire can find no oxygen.

Those who do not develop coping strategies are often cremated by it.

The first lesson in fear is to understand it better. That's why I write about it, to help others, to help myself.

Fear is pandemic. It converses in a universal tongue. There is not a shore where this invader has not landed. I know because I get letters of confirmation from across the globe. The most common question I am asked is, 'How do you manage fear?' Everyone is different of course and each feels they harbour a terror so unique that others might not (or could not) understand. So I try not to be too prescriptive when this question is proffered, I just offer (as honestly as I can) what worked (what continues to work) for me.

I have discovered on my own journey that contrary to popular belief, there are not many fears, there is only one (though it is a master of disguise). When you understand this and stop being tricked, it really helps. Suddenly, you are not dealing with an army; you are dealing with just one feeling, and if you can become desensitised to that feeling, you can overcome your fear.

First and foremost, to master fear we need exposure, and lots of it. The more the better. With this in mind it might be a good idea to become (what the poet Rumi called) a night traveller.

This is what I did (also see my book *Watch My Back*). I went out into the darkness and I hunted down my fears. It is easier, more profitable and less exhausting to attack than it is to defend.

The pre-emptive strike is consistently effective in physical, psychological, physiological and spiritual self-defence.

I discovered that, when I hunted my fears, three-dimensional monsters quickly became two-dimensional cartoons that turned to sand under my gaze.

This continues to be the case.

But – and this is important – I never overcame fear! Another big lesson for me. Initially, I was trying to find cure for fear, like it was an illness, not realising that the key was not to get rid of it, but to lose my fear of fear. Whilst I did overcome many individual fears (violence, abandonment, etc.), I found that the moment I peaked one mountain, I was automatically at the bottom of another. You might think this depressing. I find it exhilarating. Every time the weight starts to feel a little light, my Invisible Supporter slides another disc along the bar.

The universe is talking to us. It wants us to grow, and it knows that there is no growth in comfort. So when the language feels like terror, and my knees are doing an involuntary bossa nova, I remind myself of this, and I marinate in the anxiety. I bathe in it until I don't know where the fear ends and I begin. And when I centre myself, when I listen, when I tune into the fear, my enemy becomes my engine. My fear becomes my fuel.

The more fear I feel, the better I perform. So when it rears its ugly head, I go eyeball to eyeball with it. I open the door, let it in, sit it down, make it a drink and offer it some food. I sit with it until it dissipates.

The second thing I did was I wrote about my life, my fears, my journey and I spun my words across the World Wide Web. I know that as a species we all suffer from 'the forgetting' so we all need continual reminding. My words go out, they help other people (other night travellers find my notes, it serves them), they come back, they help me. They help me when I write them, they help me when I read them and they help me when I send them out into the world. The writing is also my catharsis. As you know, fear likes to prey on vulnerable minds. It likes to blackmail. I find that placing my fear in print and putting it out for the world to read stops this from happening.

We all have days when we think, 'What is this all about?'; days when that voice (or voices) in our head tells us to 'give up, it's not worth it'. This is the voice of ego. It needs to transcend. It feeds on negative attention. You kill it when you take attention away.

Here are a few other tips that I have found helpful in relation to fear.

Do the things you most fear to do. DO them. Stop talking. Put your bollocks on the table (or a female equivalent) and start experiencing. Now is the time – not tomorrow, not next week, not next year or in the New Year. Now! Life is short my friends and it is later than you think.

Meditate every day. Yoga is very good because it triggers the parasympathetic nervous system and slows the adrenals. This will make your fear more manageable.

Train till you sweat. This acts as a surrogate release for trapped adrenalin and takes the edge off excessive anxiety.

Physical training can be your salvation.

Read widely. Read books that challenge you. Knowledge helps to dispel fear. But it is unlikely to be the knowledge that you will pick up in a tabloid, or watching a soap on the TV. These things will probably only exacerbate your fear, because they are laced with negativity, and negativity triggers the adrenals.

If you think you are spiritual read *Siddhartha* by Herman Hess. If you think you are free, read Gurdjieff. If you think you are brave, check out Mahatma Gandhi. If you think you have integrity, read *The Fountainhead* by Ayn Rand.

These are just a few of the books that have helped many great men and women achieve impossible things.

Spend your money and invest in yourself. Stop being so tight. Good information is priceless. So what if it costs you silver to buy it? It cost the seller blood and sinew and that one non-refundable commodity: time! What else are you going to use your money for? If you don't invest in you, who will? People throw hundreds, even thousands of pounds at beer, takeaways and fast cars, but they will not invest in things that might transform their very existence (like books and taking instruction from men of experience). Knowledge will reap you a harvest that is worth more than Solomon's fortune.

And if you think you haven't got the money, you think too small. Work harder, earn more, or stop wasting money on the ephemeral and redirect your coffers into something infinite.

There is a lot of contradictory advice out there. Read it all. Cross-reference it with your own experience. This should tell you if it has merit. If you do not have a lot of experience, either go out there and try the information out for yourself (and be the proof) or cross-reference it with your intuition.

As a rule of thumb, if it scares the shit out of you it is probably worthy.

In my world, all red lights are green lights, large crowds walk away from the light and beaten paths lead to barren landscapes. Many great gifts come in difficult packaging. Other than that, be inspired only by people who walk their talk (never take advice on diet from a fat life coach! Never ask advice on diamonds from a brick builder), only follow your own maps and only then for a while (they will keep changing).

And the biggest lesson I have learned thus far (other than to always walk towards your fears and lean into the sharp edges) is to get off your arse and experience. And if it is a fat arse, why is it a fat arse? Do something about it (there is only so long you can keep kidding yourself that you are big boned and that 'everything I eat turns to fat'). Get out there and get uncomfortable. Growth is not meant to be easy. It is deliberately hard because knowledge demands girder-sized shoulders.

Be a man of experience (do not be an ant pretending to lead a bull) because at the end of the day experience is the only currency. And you will know when you are a man of experience because people will beat a path to your door. When you are a man of experience, people will search you out from across the globe, to seek out your advice, to heed your counsel, to bathe in your light, to be inspired by your life.

Let me tell you, people are desperate to be inspired. They are desperate for wisdom that has been born through bollock-breaking hardship. And, of course, if the dollar is your incentive, people are happy to pay top dollar for a truth if it has blood and snot as an accompaniment.

So, if you are out there now, struggling with fear, maybe it's time to change direction. Instead of moving away from the heat, why not turn into it? Go through the forge. Rather than feeling needlessly tortured for another long day of spinning and toiling, you can become the tempered blade that looks back and knows better.

Oh, and if you want to do me that huge personal favour, please send this article out to as many people as you can (because then it will come back to me – and back to you).

Just because I am the man who wrote the words, it doesn't mean that I am a man who doesn't need to read the words again.

Chapter 26

Ideas are maps

Ideas are maps! An interesting concept and true, I think. Bob Dylan said so and he is the consummate journeyman. But, from the uncensored glut, begging our attention, which ideas should we adopt? Conspiracy and royal assassination? Parental murder on some foreign shore? I think we need to be discerning about the information on offer, because whilst provocative headlines might seem artlessly incidental, if you expose yourself to them often enough they become insidiously affecting. I know. I followed these maps briefly in a former incarnation. I got a dizzy fishbowl headache and was left nauseously cynical. These ideas are maps, but the terrain is untrue and the destination is one without soul. These days I'm very particular about the notions I entertain. I am finicky over the charts I navigate. My sanity demands no less. I've learned to formulate my own ideas and follow my own maps (and even these are malleable). My own maps afford me a better viewpoint, a higher perspective. Instead of assassination and intrigue, I imagine tragic accidents in French tunnels. In place of homicidal mothers, I pray for innocent and hideously grieving parents. These benevolent maps – even if later proven inaccurate – lead me to a place of hope and compassion. And whilst I am often accused of utopianism, it's got to be better than its bleak alternative.

Chapter 27
Armstrong's Hills

Beginnings are hard.

Beginnings are always hard. I think that this is one of the reasons so many people avoid them.

People (as a general rule of thumb) tend to avoid anything that is hard, that's why they end up living unfulfilled, often unsuccessful lives. It is not because they lack potential (we all have potential), rather they lack the courage it takes to engage discomfort. And there can be no worse discomfort than those dreaded beginnings; new jobs, new schools, new diets, new books, new ventures, new homes. I love beginnings.

Actually, that is not true. I hate beginnings! That's not entirely true either. I love them, but I dread them because they are so… uncomfortable. I am currently in the process of engaging as many beginnings in my present line of work (film writing) as possible. I am doing this because I figure that, if it is the beginning of a project that I struggle with then the best thing for me to do if I want to grow as a screenwriter (as a person) is do as many as I can, so that eventually I become comfortable with the discomfort of beginnings. When I was frightened of confrontation as a younger man, I donned a tuxedo and a dicky bow and became a bouncer. This gave me exposure to a huge amount of confrontation. On a nightly (often hourly) basis someone was shouting, spitting, screaming, punching or kicking at me (but enough about my family). I flooded myself with confrontational moments and very quickly became comfortable with confrontation. In the end, it was not unusual to have some Neanderthal threatening me (it happened a million times), and all I'd say is, 'Whatever.' When I was a martial artist struggling with the grappling aspect of my training, I joined a full-time grappling club and started doing judo three times a day until I was completely comfortable with scrimmage. The beginning was a killer. But as I got used to it, I learned to love grappling. As a magazine columnist, I struggled with the concept of writing complete articles in 800 words or less. I am a man who is comfortable with 50,000 words because this gives me time to explore my subject, it gives me room to say what I want to say, it gives me room to be... what's the word? Lazy! Writing long is where I felt strong. But the magazines do not have room for long, they want short. They want you to condense the entire content of a book into a small article. I found this very hard. So, I decided to make a specialty out of short writing. I did this by working for five magazines at the same time, all demanding an original 800-word article, once a month. It was all I did and, as you can imagine, when you are writing for five magazines at the same time, you soon get very good at it. And now, as a man making his name in the hugely competitive world of screenplays, I am flooding myself (eight hours a day) with this type of writing, and (in particular) I am facing my nemesis – the blank sheet! The white (bullying) parchment that challenges me to spill a little ink and begin a new film. And because beginnings are hard, that is what I am specialising in at this moment in time. Of course, I also have to finish projects (but that has never been a problem for me), but mostly I flood myself with beginnings. I got the idea after reading about Lance Armstrong, the serial Tour de France winner. What inspired me about this great man was not just that he managed to fight cancer against horrendous odds, but also that he went on to win The Tour De France an unprecedented eight times. He won it so many times that the organisers of the race actually changed the route (I believe four times) to give the other riders a better chance of winning. What intrigued me was not so much that Lance Armstrong won the race so many times, rather it was the way in which he went about it. He looked at the Tour route and realised that the hardest part of the course, the part that every rider struggled with, was the hills. He also realised that if he could master the hills, he could dominate the whole course. So that is what he did. Whilst the other riders concentrated on their flat riding, Armstrong was on the hills, up and down again and again and again until he mastered them, until he was comfortable with them. In fact, until he loved the hills. He destroyed all the competition because he leaned into the sharp edges, he faced his fear, he worked on his weak game. So, now I use Lance Armstrong as an example and an inspiration in every new endeavour. I look long and hard and ask myself; what is the Armstrong's hill in this? What is it that everyone else is avoiding? What is it that I'm avoiding? It is a good question to ask yourself. What is the one thing in my job, my life, my sport, my relationship and my health that I (and perhaps everyone else) is avoiding because it is so tough? If you can find it, if you can face it and confront it, marinate in it, you will rise to the top very quickly because everybody else will be doing what everyone else always does: they'll be putting things off. Permanently.

People do not begin because beginnings are hard. Beginnings are always hard. Until, of course, you start to specialise in beginnings.

Chapter 28

No Shoes

I thought I was poor because I had no shoes, until I met a man who had no feet. It is an old, hackneyed (even corny) saying but it is as true today as when it was first penned at the beginning of the century when America was going through the worst depression in its short history. I like using it because it tells me that there is always someone worse off than me and that, actually, certainly in Britain, there are great opportunities for anyone with a strong work ethic and an ounce of bottle. Those who possess (what I call) the Immigrant Mentality. Let me explain. I was at the cinema a few weeks ago. I am writing films at the moment so I try to visit the pictures as often as I can to study what is working (or not) in the contemporary world of celluloid (it's a difficult job but...) As I queued for my coffee, I got talking to a Polish girl called Kasha who worked there. She told me that she was currently at Coventry University studying for a master's degree and working at the cinema to make some spare cash. She was doing forty hours a week! When I commented (with admiration) that forty hours was a lot considering that she was studying for a master's her eyes lit up and she said (quite innocently), 'But it is so easy to make money in this country. All you have to do is work.' All you have to do is work. I loved that. The simplicity. The honesty. She explained that in her country work was scarce and for those lucky enough to find employ the wages were breadline. In Britain (she said) there was lots of work and the money was great. And mostly it wasn't hard work. She said that working at the cinema making coffee, punching tickets and occasionally cleaning was no hardship. She felt as though she was getting paid most of the time just for turning up. This very healthy perspective is what I call the Immigrant Mentality. When you come from a country of poverty to a place like Britain the streets really are paved with gold. This lady has really helped me. Whenever (now) I feel as though my workload is tough and that things are not happening quickly enough or that life is unfair, I change perspectives. I allow my mind to re-visit times in my life when I had no work, no money or when I balanced three jobs just to get by. I allow myself to see my environment through the eyes of an immigrant and very quickly I start to appreciate (again) what a fantastic life I have.

Chapter 29
All Sailors

I read the newspaper and the headlines disturb me; men, women, the old and the young, boys and girls, every age, sex, denomination, colour and creed, all suffering, all in pain. People lost, people broken, people killed, people suffering and people in turmoil.

It appeared to me as though the universe *out there* was an ocean of pain and the whole world was drowning.

As I said, it upset me at first, because the very thought of people suffering is always cause for great sadness. Then I pondered on my angst and I thought back to my own periods of pain, uncertainty, jealousy, anger and greed – all times that found me neck deep in waves of discomfort – and I smiled. I realised that it was often only whilst completely submerged in my distress that I reached out for, and found, Invisible

Support. All of my major epiphanies had come from a place of darkness. My faith had found gestation in the very centre of the difficult life situations that I had been through, because it was only then, at my weakest, that I was able (in fact, that I even wanted) to access God. It was only at that point of compete submergence, when the ego had abandoned ship, when all outside help had been exhausted or was not forthcoming and I felt drowning was an imminent certainty, that I opened up to Other means of support. It was only in my darkest hour that I was able to reach God.

Then I heard the song 'Suzanne', written and performed by Leonard Cohen. The lyrics deeply moved me. In fact, they offered me great solace because they paralleled and validated my own experience. The words suggested that salvation came (as Dante said) 'neither from the cushion nor the bed', rather they were delivered from the crucifix of difficulty. Wisdom does not come from a Christmas cracker; sapience is born from hard experience. The words of the song said: 'And Jesus was a sailor, when he walked upon the water, and he spent a long time watching from his lonely wooden tower, and when he knew for certain only drowning men could see him, He said, "All men will be sailors then. Until the sea shall free them." '

The lyrics were balm because they allowed me to see purpose behind my pain, and a purpose behind other people's pain. I realised that whilst I have massive compassion for the suffering (of myself and others), I am also filled with hope because I have faith that in his (your, my) darkest hour the drowning man can see God. We are all sailors and we all suffer the inclemency of the ocean, not because the sea is cruel, but rather because the sea can save us, but not until we are drowning.

So if you are drowning right now my prayers and my love go out to you, but they are juxtaposed by massive faith that all will be well. So hold on in there, it will not last forever, nothing does, nothing can. I also offer and attach to that prayer my congratulations, because even though you might think that your suffering is needless torture, I know that the drowning is the very beginning of your salvation.

Reach out and ask for help and know that it will come.

Be well.

Chapter 30

Difficult-difficult, Difficult-easy

I bumped into an old friend from the distant past. In my early days as a hard-nosed knuckle-dragger he was one of my compatriots, and one of the hardest-working martial artists around. He had always prided himself on his sinewy mentality when it came to all things physical, and he had a prolific work rate. After a brief (and predictable) catch up (how's the work, the car, the kids, the wife and the mum – in that order) he said, 'Hey, you still doing 'animal day'?'

Animal day, for those who do not know, is a form of knockout or submission fighting (any range, any technique) that I pioneered in the mad, bad (and often sad) 1990's. It was a time I absolutely loved, but a time I am also grateful to have left behind.

I shook my head in the negative. It had been many years since I engaged in my last animal day fight.

'Why not?' he asked, adding, 'I'm still mad for it.'

'Because it is difficult-easy,' I said, 'and in order for me to continue growing my character, I don't need difficult-easy. In order for me to grow my character I need difficult-difficult.'

He gave me one of those loud, squinty-eyed, confused looks that shouted from a hundred feet, 'Explain!'

So I explained.

Even as a veteran of thousands of fights, animal days were still a scary experience for me. They were violent and dangerous and extremely difficult. But because I had fought so many times and knew the terrain well, it no longer stretched me. Whatever it was that I needed to reap from that hard period of my life had been well-and-truly harvested. There was nothing left for me to learn there. Animal day was still difficult, and from the outside looking in it probably looked as though it was mad difficult, but for me it wasn't. In fact, it had become difficult-easy.

My friend was still in love with the ground-and-pound-style fighting and whilst his physical prowess was evident, he had not grown even a single inch in any other area of his life, probably not for the last ten years. His was the mistake made by many; they presume that if something is difficult then they are in the arena. But experience has taught me that the only time you are truly in the arena is when you are (ever so slightly) out of your depth.

Difficult-easy is when you are on familiar terrain, no matter how hard the going.

Difficult-difficult is when you find yourself at the bottom of someone else's class with three crazy training partners, fear at your left, doubt on your right and (that big bastard) uncertainty squaring up in front of you.

Difficult-easy is treading water whilst kidding yourself that you are swimming against the tide.

Difficult-difficult doesn't need to employ pretence because it is drowning and swimming for its life.

I see many people suffering stalled development because they are so busy occupying themselves with very worthy, respectably difficult-easy tasks that they use to avoid the difficult-difficult areas of their lives.

I am doing it right now as it happens. I should be doing a rewrite of a difficult-difficult film script that is overdue, but instead I am busying myself with a piece of difficult-easy work that is not really due to be in print for another fortnight (damn!)

Some (more) examples: you bury your relationship problems (difficult-difficult) under hundreds of miles of road running (difficult-easy).

You fill every spare moment with hard lists of worthy causes (difficult-easy) so that you don't have the time to invest in the book that you were always going to write, or the film you would love to make (if only you were not so committed in other areas) or the (difficult... very difficult) painting career that you had always intended to create.

You immerse yourself in course after course, book after book (so difficult, and yet... so deliciously easy) on becoming a life coach/ property developer/ master chef instead of just getting out there (difficult, oh so difficult) and actually doing it.

Listen. Let me tell you, the moment a task becomes difficult-easy you stop growing. That is a fact. In order to re-establish your vital development you need to take an honest inventory (difficult, very difficult – I have done it) of your life, ditch the pretence and embrace the black that is... difficult-difficult.

It doesn't necessarily mean that we lose all the difficult-easy things in our life: one or two are OK (they might even be fun), some of them probably bring us revenue and even offer vital respite. But in order to grow (and we are in the business of growth) we need a constant influx of difficult-difficult tasks in our life.

So... stop chasing ostentatious challenges (that are difficult-easy for you) and sort out your health; you are three stone overweight and your blood pressure is off the scale.

Kill the worthy endeavours that you believe other people will think are impressive and do something truly and uniquely impressive; take your (secret) addictions to task and kill the porn (in all its forms).

Stop collecting trophies and certificates and belts that tell the word how successful you are and actually BE a success, by taking a hammer to that creepily burgeoning fear that you are harbouring.

And don't, please (like my old mate) fall into the trap of mistaking hard work – even extremely hard (easy) work – for progress. Because, let's be frank, difficult-easy is really just another way of saying 'easy', and there is no growth in easy.

We aspirants are into the hard game, the long game, the difficult-difficult game. What we are not into, or what we should never be into, is the game of easy.

Chapter 31

Enlightenment, Please – But Not Just Yet!

Lord! God Almighty. (The universe).

A word if thy will.

A word about me.

Actually, more precisely, a word about me and my specious requests.

When I beg you for, 'Enlightenment now!' without gestation or acclimatisation, know that I ask for more weight than I can currently hold. Please just proffer time and patience in its place and when I complain and complain (as I am apt to complain) that, 'Lord, but I am ready,' I beg you to know that I am not ready. If I was so sure of myself I would not need to talk all the time.

And when I call for clement weather send me instead a north wind, the same wind you sent the

Vikings. The wind that made the Vikings will surely make me.

And whilst talking of Vikings, when I ask for the warrior's sword and armour, send me in its place a warrior's journey and a mapless terrain that will layer fold over fold to my spirit. Because it is the hard passage that sculpts fine character, and setting our own course that inspires wisdom. Everything else is ostentation.

And Almighty, when this journey brings me to doubt (which it must) and I plead for certainty, please pretend that You misheard me and guide me instead toward faith, where to know that there is too much to know is to know enough.

And on this long journey, Lord, I know that tiredness will call and *him fallen* will rest upon my weary back and whisper promises of ascension before the fortieth day. Sojourn me in the place of misery and wickedness if even a breath separates his tender from my negation, guide me home through Your narrow gate because what he calls the wide gate I know to be death.

And when I ask for tomorrow's due today because today's seems a meagre store (and I will ask), please retreat me back to yesterday's poverty so as I might better appreciate my current abundance: the present bliss.

And when bliss and difficulty swap their turn (as they are sure to do) and I plead for escape, please plunge me deeper into the forge that I might later emerge, if not a tempered blade at least a better man.

Judging also is not my strong suit, Master, so when I point at others' splinters please ram another mote in my eye and place me before my own reflection.

And when I look for lottery (as I always look for lottery), bring me not the loot of Solomon, just a looking glass will suffice and a reminder that *I Am that I Am*. Because I Am is all the fortune I need.

And one more thing, Great Christos. Before I suffer yet another forgetting: if I keep making cloy my hanker, especially when I already have so much and others have so little, give it to me, satisfy my glut! Drown me in diamonds and pearls, carriages and caravans of precious metal, gift me talents and homes beyond my count, shower me with titles and honours and accolades cast in gold. Because if I keep asking for added worth without at least proffering further service then I deserve the road of the wicked, dark as night. That is surely where this greed will bring me.

Perhaps then along Blake's road of excess I might, finally, find my palace of wisdom, the righteous road getting brighter and brighter until daylight comes.

www.summersdale.com
www.geoffthompson.com